relax

Today more and more people are becoming aware of the part that stress and tension play in illness and in lowering morale, and following the relaxation programmes on Radio 4's *You and Yours* there were many enquiries for a written guide.

Here is that guide: a clear and concise outline of the art of relaxation through muscle control. The author gives a plan which, if followed through, will result in the user being able to relax at will. Further chapters cover the use of relaxation techniques in everyday life, and show how the rest of the family can help.

Knowing how to relax is invaluable in the prevention of stress, it will induce calm and relieve fatigue: moreover it is entirely under your own control.

relax

the relief of tension
through muscle control

Jane Madders

illustrated by Richard Bonson

British Broadcasting Corporation

Published by the British Broadcasting Corporation,
35 Marylebone High Street, London W1M 4AA

ISBN 0 563 12464 4

First published 1973

© Jane Madders 1973

Set and printed in Great Britain by
Tonbridge Printers Ltd, Peach Hall Works,
Tonbridge, Kent

Contents

Foreword	6
Introduction	8
1 Why Relax?	11
2 How to Relax	22
3 Full Relaxation	42
4 How a Partner Can Help	49
5 Pre-menstrual Tension and the Menopause	58
6 Putting it into Practice	68
7 Relaxation for Living	71
8 Quick Reference Guide	78
9 Book List	80

Foreword

'For as long as I can remember I've been told "Relax", but no one has ever told me how!'

That was the beginning of one of the many letters which came to *You and Yours* when we broadcast Jane Madders' series on relaxation. Almost every letter said in one way or another how useful it was to have such practical and simple ideas to work on, and this seemed to us one of the most important features of the series.

Anyone can use this method to some degree at least – there is no mystique about it, and it is meant to be part of an ordinary life, whether you work at home, in an office, factory, or wherever.

Jane Madders has plenty of qualifications to teach relaxation: she's a qualified teacher of physical education, a chartered physiotherapist and a lecturer at a college of education. But as well as qualifications she has a lot of experience to build on – she has taught relaxation for several years to pregnant mothers, to athletes, to migraine sufferers and to students. It is no surprise that with this background listeners found her talks helped with a whole range of tensions and bodily ills.

While I was working on the series I talked to some people who had been to relaxation classes a year or more before I met them. What they had to say made it very clear that the benefits of learning to relax had lasted, and become an important part of their lives. Here are some examples:

'My doctor kept telling me to relax and I knew he was right but I simply didn't know how. Now since I've practised it my blood pressure is down to normal, he says, and I feel much calmer.'

'I have found that in driving, especially going to work in the city, I am much more relaxed when I get to work. Now when I arrive I am a lot fresher and don't feel I've done a day's work by the time I get through the traffic.'

'I suffered badly from insomnia and had very large doses of sleeping tablets for over twenty years but I still wasn't sleeping properly. Now I hardly ever have anything and am sleeping much better than before.'

We hoped that listeners to the series would also find lasting help from it. However, it's not always possible to be near your radio when you want to be – or to remember every word you hear. We had one postcard which complained that someone came in while the writer was listening, and 'I missed the arms and legs.'

Plenty of people who were luckier and heard the whole series wanted to have Jane Madders' ideas written down, so they could refer to them whenever they wanted. And a lot of wives who were themselves helped by the programme, felt like this one who wrote: 'As my husband is at work during the day it is impossible for him to hear your programme on relaxation and I feel he is missing out on something that could change his life in a very positive way.'

The letters we received all added up to a powerful plea for the publication of this book – which we believe *does* offer you something very positive.

Jocelyn Ryder-Smith
Producer, Features and Documentaries.

Introduction

'Relax!' It is likely that someone has said this to you or you have urged someone else to do it and with little effect. Although we are continually being reminded of the ill effects of excessive tension and may well be aware of it in ourselves, we are rarely shown just *how* to relax.

Perhaps the word relax gives the wrong impression, because to some people this may mean having a good time or to others mere passive flopping. What I shall describe is active, conscious muscle control, ways of recognising unnecessary muscle tension and of how to release this when you wish. It is something which can be incorporated into daily living and can be learnt by everyone to some degree. It involves no meditation, hypnotic suggestion, difficult postures or exercises.

For some years it has been recognised that prolonged stress, whether it is caused by anxiety, fatigue, injury or periods of high arousal, can trigger off a number of diseases. Some of these can be killers, and others, while they do not destroy life, can often ruin it.

There is a very close relationship between muscle tension and emotional states, and this book is an attempt to explain this simply and to describe a method of releasing tension by relaxation techniques. Relaxation can induce a feeling of calm, reduce fatigue and affect some of the internal workings of the body so that the churning dies down. This is something you can do for yourself, and as it uses no drugs, it is under your control. It is more useful as a regularly-practised preventative against stress rather than a measure introduced at cracking point, but doctors may advise relaxation techniques as a useful addition to other medical treatment.

There is nothing abnormal about tension, anxiety or fatigue. These are necessary for successful living, but when they become excessive, prolonged and unnecessary, the body reacts in protest.

I began teaching relaxation many years ago when I held classes for women who were learning to relax as part of their antenatal preparation for childbirth. However, once they had had their babies the mothers found that they needed help with relaxation even more, when short of sleep, or irritable because the babies don't behave as the books say they should.

So we formed a Family Club, based on relaxation and group discussion. Among the members were some who were suffering from disorders associated with stress: insomnia, gastric ulcers, high blood pressure, asthma and migraine. A local consultant from a migraine clinic contacted me and I began classes for men and women suffering from this wretched complaint. Although there are other factors besides stress which trigger off migraine attacks, the effects of group relaxation therapy were so promising, and in some cases spectacular, that other teachers were trained in this method and more classes held.

Some of these classes were extended to include people referred by their doctors because they were suffering from other stress disorders.

More recently, as a lecturer at a college of education, I included relaxation as a skill worth learning by teachers and students to combat the increasing stress of life.

1 Why Relax?

Some doubts and certainties

Some people say yes, but ... when the idea of relaxation as a self-help measure is first put to them. They say that they would like to relax, but they are just too busy. Or, they had tried it once and they were hopeless because they are tense by nature. Others say they can't see how flapping arms about can possibly help a headache, and in any case it is the *mind* that needs relaxing. And some people are so terrified of visiting the dentist that they are frozen in their fear and are convinced that nothing could help them.

This healthy scepticism is a good start because to be really effective, relaxation techniques must be based on the kind of conviction which comes from understanding and experience. I'll try to deal with these doubts later, but first we must be clear what relaxation cannot do and what it can. Pain and worry are useful warnings that something is wrong. Relaxation will neither remove problems nor can it cure disease that requires medical or surgical treatment.

But there are a number of things it *can* do and this is supported by evidence from studies in a number of countries, though there may be some variations in the methods used. When you are practising it is worth while reminding yourself of the ways in which it can be useful:

You can use it as a weapon against stress

Remember that 'stress' has a wider meaning than anxiety and overwork. It can also mean over-alertness, high levels of arousal, anything which the body interprets as threatening. This includes such widely differing things as noise, criticism and major changes in life patterns. Hans Selye has said that even sheer joy is enough to activate the bodily stress mechanism to some extent. But it isn't the situation itself that produces the ill effects, it is our reaction to it, and it is this that relaxation can help to control. Experience has shown that if you can voluntarily relax your muscles you attain a sensation of relaxation in your mind also, and there is a definite relationship between the extent of this muscle relaxation and a state of calm. Some people will find it harder to learn than others and some situations will make it exceptionally difficult, but I have never found anyone who didn't improve at least a little and even a small step forward helps. As you learn you will know yourself better so that you become aware of how much stress you can take and plan accordingly.

Use it to combat fatigue

You may have been unaware of unnecessary muscle tension in daily living and this will all add to fatigue. To relax you must first recognise tension, and the learning exercises (including the relaxed arm swinging which isn't really *flapping*) are to help you recognise the difference between a working muscle and a relaxed one and to give a feeling of looseness. You can drop the exercises later when you can relax at will.

Use it to cope with pain

Relaxation can make pain hurt *less* whereas tension will exaggerate it. Relaxation in the dentist's chair makes treatment much more manageable ... for the dentist as well as the patient, and it can be used in other situations where some pain is expected or is inevitable. Its use in childbirth has been known for years, but it requires a somewhat different training and practice to apply it to everyday situations.

Use it to improve your performance of physical skills

Unnecessary tension impedes effective performance whether it is in games or work. The effortless grace and ease of great dancers and athletes is the result of co-ordinated control of muscle so that the maximum result is obtained with the minimum of effort. Unrecognised muscle tension in one area of the body may make all the difference between a humdrum performance and a highly skilled one.

Use it to help your relationships with others

People warm to someone who is calm and relaxed, and when you are, you will find that you are able to listen with compassion rather than with anger in difficult situations. When you are relaxed, your voice and manner helps those around to drop their tensions too. But when the time comes for you to be forceful, you can give it all you have got with dramatic results, and you can simmer down quickly afterwards with no ill effects.

1 The Bodily Effects of Stress

If you are a worrier, and I expect that some of you are, it is no use for people to say to you: 'Don't worry, there's nothing to worry about', because you do and so there is. It is well-meant but futile advice. Indeed, worry may serve a useful purpose, for it enables us to think round a problem, mentally trying out this and that way of solving it until we come up with an answer. It is when it becomes no longer the trigger to action but a permanent state that the bodily effects are disabling and harmful.

It is now recognised that emotional states, especially when they persist for long periods, can have profound effects on the body, sometimes damaging the organs or predisposing them to infection. Different people react in different ways to stress and excitement. Your inherited tendencies and your personality characteristics acquired early in life will influence your reaction. Some people respond more sensitively to every stimulus – to bright lights, loud noises, strong smells, changes in environment and to other people. They are bombarded with sensations, are on the alert all the time, and may be addicted to work and feel guilty when things are not achieved. Other people seem never to have enough excitement, see fewer situations as alarming and need a good push to get them steamed up. All these are not better or worse people, they are just different, and some are more vulnerable than others.

Just as people are different in their response to situations, so their bodies react in ways which are special to the individual. Some, for instance, will have headaches as a result of stress, others gastric or bowel upsets, high blood pressure, skin rashes, asthma – we all have our individual pattern of response. (There are of course other causes for these disorders but most are triggered off by stress). All these reactions have one thing in common. They are the result of the body's defence reaction to threat.

Like all animals, man has an in-built survival mechanism which enables him to act efficiently when his life is threatened. As soon as danger is perceived the muscles tense, and the message is received by the brain. The part of the brain which is the centre for the emotions is the hypothalamus. It is concerned with the harmonious integration of all the systems involved in maintaining the internal balance necessary for survival. When the message of danger

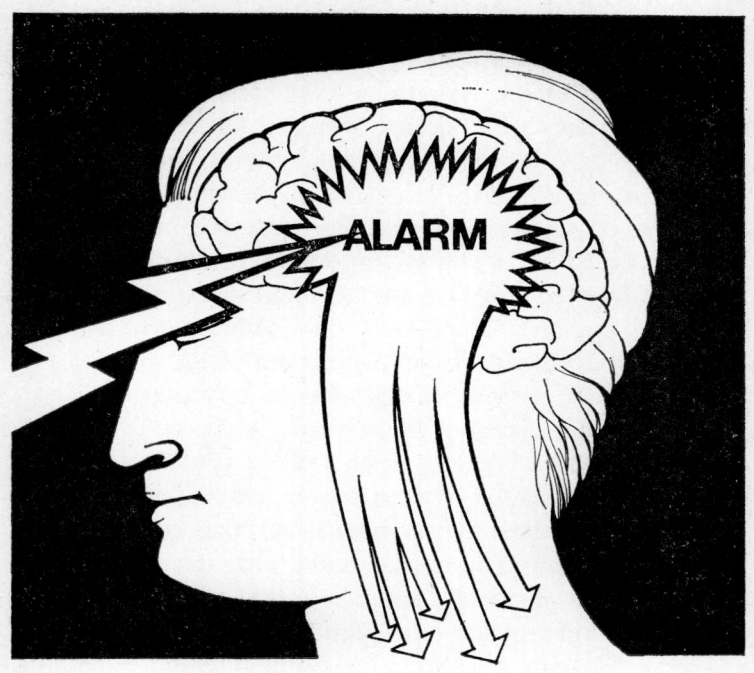

is received, it goes into action.

Suppose, for example, you were about to be attacked by a hooligan in a dark street. Immediately you realise this, it is as if the panic button in your brain were pressed and in a split second an amazing series of events occurs. Chemicals are shot into the bloodstream and this causes many other changes to prepare the body for action in either Flight or Fight. The whole body is mobilised to enable you to cope with attack or running away.

The heart beats more quickly and blood pressure is raised so that more blood can be pumped to the muscles, the heart and the brain. Breathing is faster, so that more oxygen reaches the muscles. Adrenalin is released from the adrenal glands and this keeps the emergency reactions going. Sugar is released from the liver to provide fuel for the working muscles. The spleen discharges its content of concentrated blood corpuscles, the abdominal muscles tighten to protect the organs. Sweating begins, so that the body may cool down in vigorous activity, and there are changes in the electrical resistance in the skin. There is an alteration of sodium and potassium balance in the blood. Because digestion is not so important for the time being, blood is diverted from the stomach and digestion is slowed down or stopped. Sometimes these effects are counter-balanced and instead of blood pressure rising, it drops and fainting occurs; instead of digestive activity ceasing it acts excessively and there may be nervous diarrhoea.

Many of these changes occur before you have time to think. As soon as the danger is over and the emotion has been discharged into action, relaxation takes place and the body quickly returns to normal and no harm is done.

But humans are unlike animals in that we have a highly developed forebrain and a brilliant creative imagination and memory. We can be scared or excited about something which is going to happen in the future and we can recall with emotion events which occurred in the past. We can also produce these alarm reactions for events which are not a threat to life itself but to our self-esteem; for situations when physical action is either inappropriate or impossible.

When this happens, the body is prepared for action when there can be no action; we summon the fire engines when there is no fire. All the physical and chemical changes meant for an emergency are maintained inappropriately for long periods. A driver fuming at traffic delays, a worker humiliated by his boss, a speaker anxious about a public occasion, a student facing an examination, a mother at screaming point with her children, all show the same Fight or Flight reactions. When these are prolonged with continued high blood pressure, digestive disturbance and all

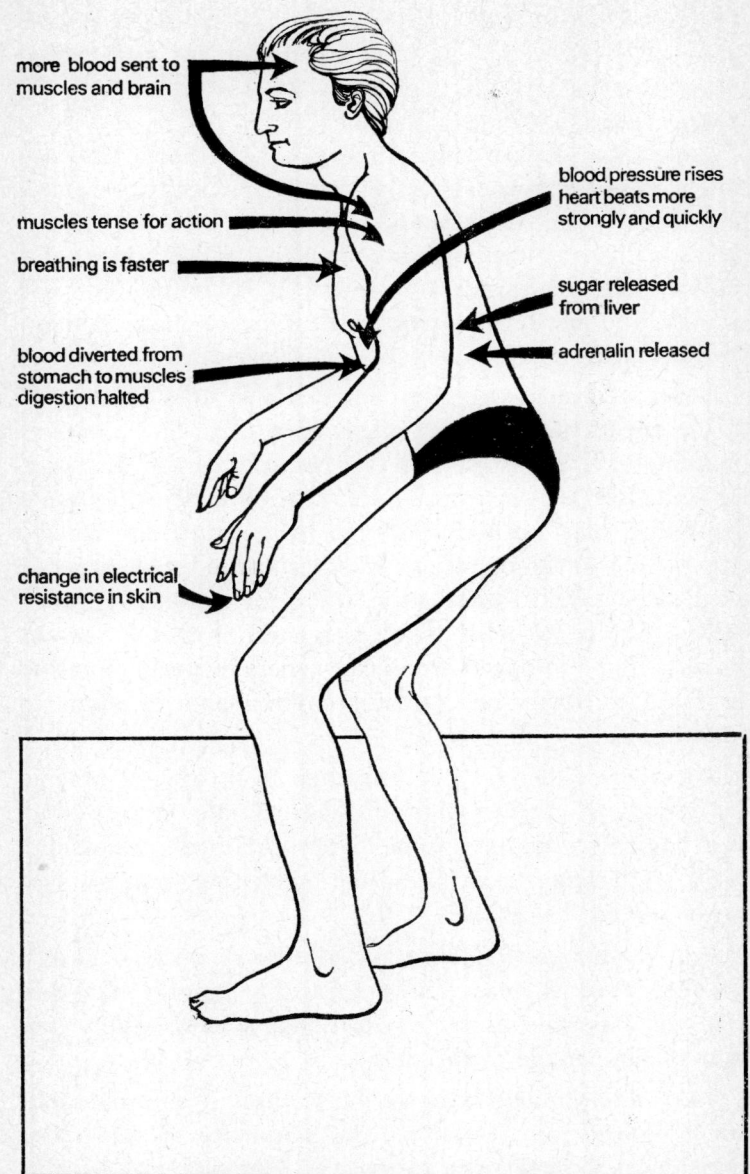

the other changes, sleep is disturbed, various real disorders may occur and man can literally stew in his own juices. There is evidence too that when stress is prolonged the body is less able to resist infection.

Relaxation as part of preparation for childbirth has been taught in this country since the 1930's. The techniques have now been more fully studied, and are used in various forms of therapy in psychiatric medicine. It has been shown that a state of muscle relaxation is incompatible with anxiety, and more recent work has confirmed that voluntary control can be exerted over some internal states.

Hans Selye made a great contribution to our knowledge of the effects of stress, and in his book, *The Stress of Life* he refers to stress as the rate of wear and tear on the body. He put forward his theory of the General Adaptation Syndrome, that the body responds in the same non-specific way to *all* kinds of stress, whether caused by excessive heat, cold, physical exhaustion, injury or emotion. He concludes that if we wish to be protected from the various diseases that prolonged stress can generate, we must either be removed from the stressful environment or learn to relax.

One answer therefore, is to escape from what is causing the stress – to change your job, leave home, change your environment. Usually this is inappropriate or impossible, but even if change is achieved the underlying problem may not be solved.

Another way is to take tranquillising or sedative drugs, but there is an increasing awareness that far too many are used unnecessarily and they have side effects which vary from one individual to another.

The more difficult way is the natural one, relaxation. Some people are put off by the simplicity of relaxation techniques; the exercises are easy to learn but need determination to put them into practice and courage to rely on them. Relaxation will not alter your situation but it will affect your reaction to it. There are no side affects, it gives you a feeling of well-being, and it is under your control and no one else's. It enhances mental awareness instead of dulling it, is a skill which will stay with you all your life, and costs nothing.

2 Muscle Tension and Fatigue

A certain amount of muscle tension is necessary during the day in order to maintain posture and keep some sort of facial expression. You would fall over if you were completely relaxed, and if ever you try taking off all the expression on your face when you are in public you will soon find that people wonder what on earth is wrong. However, a great deal of unconscious muscle tension is not only unnecessary but can be fatiguing and harmful in its results.

As you are reading this it is quite possible that you are working physically very hard. Your shoulders may be tight, the muscles hunched and hard, your jaw clenched, your forehead furrowed or your legs may be held tightly together and your abdominal muscles drawn in so strongly that your stomach aches with the effort. All this is using as much energy as if you were doing strong manual work. Yet all you are doing is sitting and 'resting'.

When a muscle is working it shortens and contracts. To do this it uses certain foods as fuel and these are broken down by chemical processes to produce energy, heat and waste products. These fatigue products, mainly lactic acid, are then cleared away in the bloodstream when the muscle relaxes.

With the normal harmony of muscle action, as one group

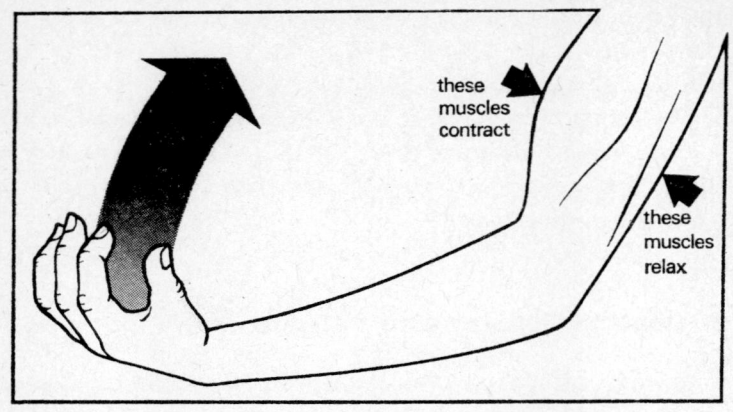

contracts, the opposing group relaxes to allow movement to take place. If the opposing group of muscles do not relax but contract also, movement cannot take place. When muscles are held tight like this (and you probably are doing this somewhere now) blood pressure is raised, circulation in the blood vessels is impeded and there is no relaxation period to aid the clearing away of the fatigue waste products.

In a rhythmical movement, like walking, there is an alternate contraction and relaxation of many groups of muscles and all the normal recovery processes continue. This explains why gentle rhythmical movement induces relaxation and relieves fatigue. But when muscles are kept in a state of contraction for prolonged periods, sometimes all day, fatigue builds up and you are more tired at the end of the day than you should be.

In addition to increasing fatigue the muscles may go into a cramp-like spasm, and this produces the sore tender muscles that are familiar to many tense people. This is particularly noticeable in the anti-gravity muscles of the neck and the spine near the shoulders.

It used to be said that muscles are always in a state of

mild contraction, but we now know that this is incorrect. When muscles are really relaxed there is no activity at all. So it *is* possible to relax them completely.

Unnecessary muscle tension can impede manual dexterity and the performance of physical skills. We can see how a tense person is unable to move with ease and grace. Dancers, athletes, games players, singers and actors are among those who incorporate relaxation into their training, and many a golf swing has been improved by eliminating unnecessary muscle tension. Relaxation is also used to aid a quick recovery after strenuous activity.

By relaxing at intervals, and being aware of unnecessary muscle tension you can save your energy for the things that really matter.

To sum this up simply:

It is tension in your muscles that first signals danger. When you relax your muscles, you begin to feel calm. To do this you must be able to recognise when muscles are tense (many people are quite unaware of this), and what it feels like when they relax. It is concerned with feeling rather than with doing, and is something which you can eventually learn.

2 How to Relax

Before you begin to practise

Learning how to relax is like acquiring any other physical skill, and everyone can learn it, some better than others. You will not be asked to conjure up beautiful images, and it does not involve meditation, hypnosis, or mere flopping, though all these do include some relaxation. Instead you will learn to become aware of muscle sensations, to recognise unnecessary muscle tension and to release it at will. The techniques are not really 'exercises', but I use the word for want of a better one.

If you were learning to drive or play the piano you would first require some strong motivation to learn – if you are going to do well you must have a good reason for trying – and you would need some basic understanding of the principles involved. Then you would have to practise over and over again until it became a habit. The same applies to relaxation. Eventually it will become incorporated into daily living and the preliminary exercises will be unnecessary except as an aid to 'winding down' when you have been under unusual pressure.

In learning to feel the difference in degrees of muscle tension you will find it an advantage to learn with other people or with a partner, but you still can do a great deal on your own. Each set of exercises should be practised for a week before moving on to the next. Don't try to gobble the whole lot at one go. It takes about six weeks or more to learn so don't expect results immediately. You will however quite soon recognise unnecessary muscle tension, and feel some benefit from controlled relaxation.

Although you should eventually be able to relax despite noise or discomfort, it is difficult to do so if you are cold. So practise in a warm room and wear comfortable unrestricting clothing.

Calm Breathing

When you are anxious or over-alert, you may find that your breathing is high in your chest, faster and more irregular than usual. At the same time you may be tightening your abdominal muscles almost as if you were expecting a blow to your stomach, and sometimes these muscles ache with the effort.

By taking a few, calm, easy breaths, letting your abdominal muscles relax and rise as you do so you can induce a feeling of calm.

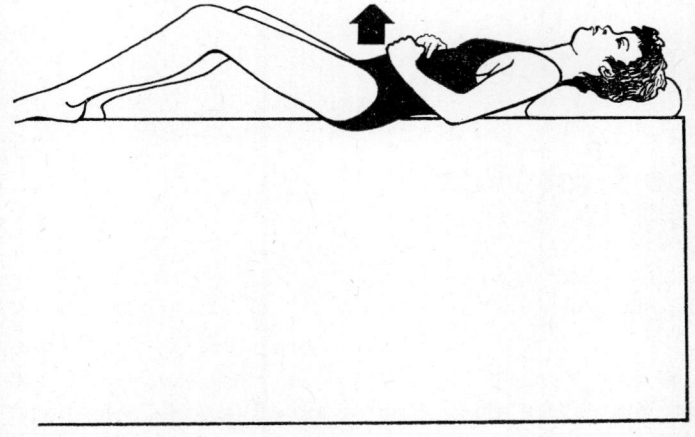

To learn this, either sit well-supported in your chair, or better still, lie on the floor on your back with your knees bent and your feet on the ground. Rest your hands lightly on your abdomen – on the bulge if you've got one – with your fingers just touching. Breathe in, and let your abdomen rise so that your hands separate a little as they rise too. Breathe out with a soft sigh and feel that you are letting go, that the tension is released and your hands and abdomen lower. Do this a few times easily and calmly in the rhythm that suits you best. Then forget about it.

When to use this kind of breathing

Begin all your relaxation practice with this kind of breathing. Use it if you are about to face a difficult situation like an interview, the dentist, speaking in public, and use it to simmer down after a row or after other events which have been stressful.

If you are one of those people who very much dislike injections try taking a deep breath just before the needle goes in, then breathe out *slowly* and relax as it is being done. You will find you feel little discomfort.

The First Week

Shoulders

Most people show their tension in shoulder muscles and these sometimes remain contracted all day. As a result they

become aching and sore, and women especially may find that carrying a heavy shopping bag is an additional strain.

To recognise what a muscle is like when it is tense and contracted put one hand across to the top of the opposite arm on the outside near the shoulder.

Raise that arm sideways a little and you will feel the muscle go tight and hard under your hand. That is a working contracted muscle, and it is using up food to produce energy, and waste fatigue products. Now let your arm drop limply to your side and feel the difference. It is soft and you can get hold of handfuls of it. That is a relaxed resting muscle.

The next exercise will help you to recognise when your shoulders are unnecessarily tense.

Hunch your shoulders right up towards your ears. The muscles are tight. Stop contracting these muscles and let them relax as you drop your shoulders. Do the same thing again, but this time tighten up only the amount you do if you are alert or anxious. Recognise this as tension, and then let go. (You will find how a partner can help you relax shoulders in chapter four.)

Combine the breathing exercise with relaxation of shoulders. Sit well back in your chair and take a few calm easy breaths, and as you do this relax your shoulders, especially as you breathe out. Sit quietly with your

shoulders relaxed and enjoy the sensation of relaxing for a few minutes in this way.

During the week
Try to notice when your shoulders are particularly tense and let them relax. You can do this when you are driving, sitting at work, doing household jobs like peeling the potatoes, watching television and when you are resting.

If you are carrying a heavy load of shopping, divide it so that you are evenly balanced, use a sling bag over your shoulder or a rucksack, or use a wheeled basket.

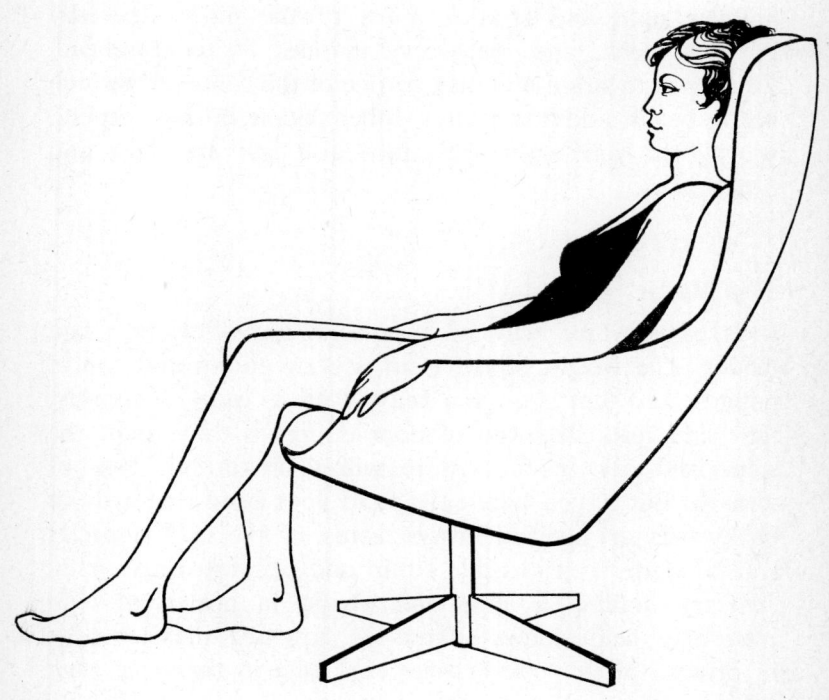

The Second Week

Face and Neck

There is a very close link between feelings and the muscles of the face. Much of our communication with people is non-verbal, especially through facial expression and the way we move the head. Usually there is constant muscle activity, with contraction alternating with relaxation so there is no strain, and there are many people whose lively wrinkled faces are the unique expression of their personality. This is quite different from those who hold their muscles tight and strained most of the time, especially the jaw, neck, and the worry muscles of the forehead. This leads to strain and may be one of the causes of tension headache. In addition to this, other people do not respond warmly to you when your face and jaw are tight and contained.

The Neck

It is easy to see why neck muscles are often sore and tender. The weight of the head is between ten and twelve pounds, and that is quite a heavy load to carry. Normally, the head rests balanced without effort on the top of the spine and easy good posture will maintain this lack of tension. But if you habitually hold your head forwards or backwards or tilted sideways, some of the neck muscles will be under considerable strain and this will cause pain. Just try holding a ten-pound weight in one hand with your arm held sideways and see how the muscles ache in protest. Your neck muscles can react in the same way.

There is special strain on the top of the spine if the head is held retracted backwards.

You can feel the neck muscles contract when you do this:

Tilt your head a little way backwards and put one hand at the back of your neck to get hold of a handful of muscle. It is like picking up a kitten by the scruff of the neck, and the muscles should feel soft. Keep hold and gradually bend your head forwards until you feel the muscles go tight and hard as they take the weight of your head. These are working, contracting muscles.

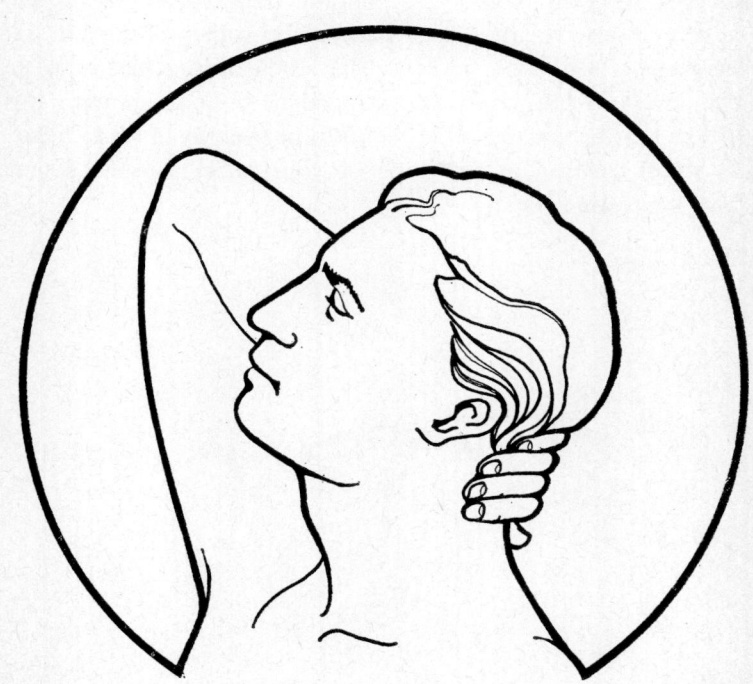

You can give yourself some neck massage to relieve tension and aid the circulation if you have been doing work that involves close concentration with head tilted forwards. Tilt your head back just a little and take hold of a handful of the muscle at the back of your neck. Squeeze and let go alternately, moving your hand gradually upwards towards your head. With the fingers of both hands make circular movements each side of your spine moving up towards the base of the skull. This is particularly useful if you have been driving for long periods or doing jobs like typing. When you have finished, move your head from side to side and forwards and backwards. Try to hold your head on a long neck without tilting it back.

If you get an aching neck avoid long periods of reading or working with your head bending forward; break off for a few moments and give your neck some movement or massage. Prop your book so that the reading matter is at eye level or rest your chin cupped in your hand with the elbow resting on the table to take the weight of your head. A small cushion at the nape of your neck is useful when you are resting.

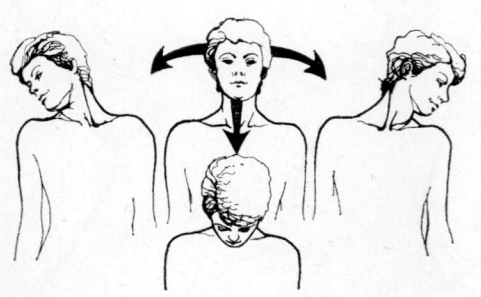

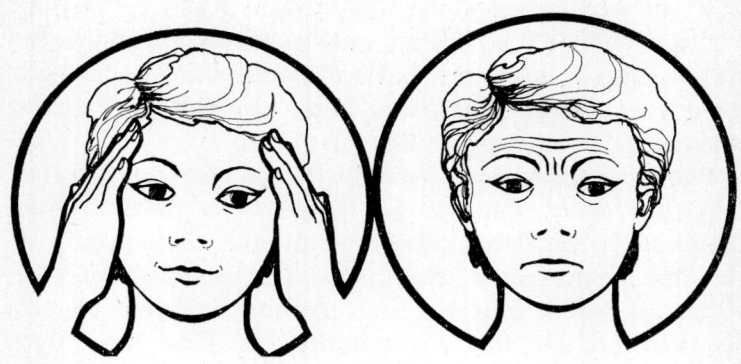

The Jaw

Many people hold their teeth clenched with jaw muscles tight for long periods during the day and even during the night as well. The next exercise will show you how easily this can lead to unnecessary strain and headache.

Put your hands at each side of your forehead just above the temples where the hair line begins. Clench your teeth and let go several times and feel how these muscles tighten to hard ridges. Let your jaw sag a little and feel the difference.

The Forehead

Much of our emotion is expressed by the muscles of the forehead. Frowning represents the aggressive Fight reaction and raising the eyebrows indicates the surprise, Flight reaction. Now if you do these both together ... it looks a bit comic, but try it facing a mirror ... you will see that you have an expression of anguish, of conflict, when you are caught in a situation when you can neither attack or withdraw. It is the 'Freeze' reaction.

If you keep your muscles like this in a state of tension for long periods you will not only look worried and signal the message to everyone, but will contribute to your own anxiety and tension headache. You can give help to the muscles by giving massage like this:

Put your fingers in the middle of your forehead so that they just meet. Smooth gently outwards towards your temples. Go on doing this smoothly and rhythmically so that the vertical lines relax. Now change and move your hands alternately upwards from the bridge of your nose to the hairline. Do this rhythmically and close your eyes softly as you do so and be aware of the sensation of a relaxed forehead. When you open your eyes try to keep that feeling.

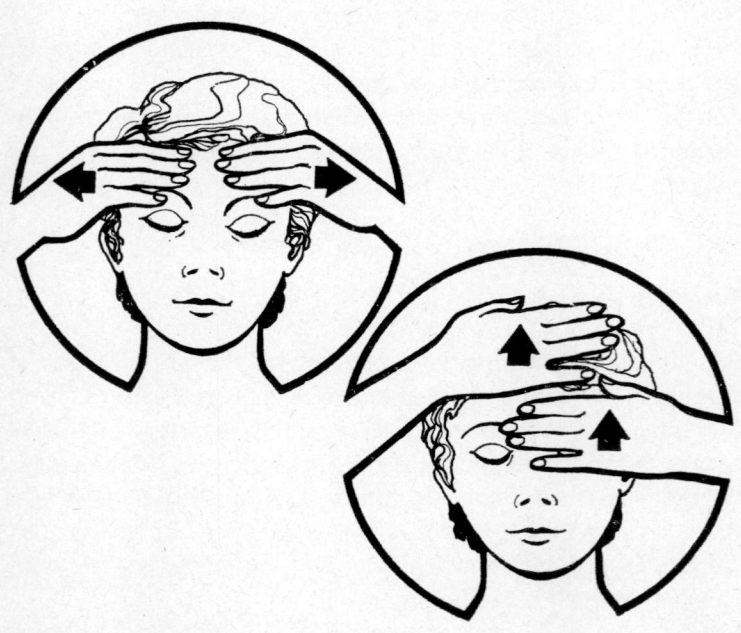

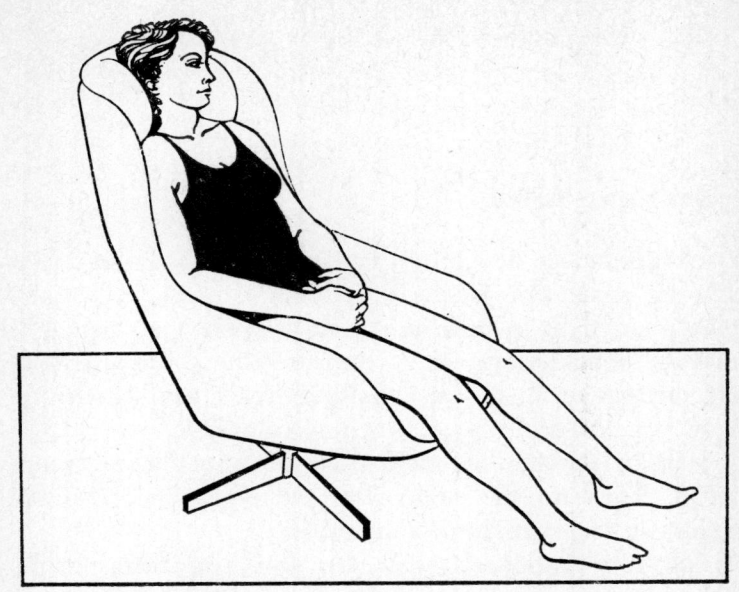

Now link this with the previous exercises:
Sit well back on your chair so that your back, thighs and, if you have a high chair, your neck are supported. Let your arms rest either on the side of the chair or put your hands on your lap without gripping your fingers. Take a few easy breaths, relaxing deliberately as you do so. Let your shoulders, arms and hands relax. Make sure your teeth are not tightly together and your forehead as smooth as when you were stroking it. Close your eyes softly and enjoy the feeling of calm and tranquillity for a few minutes.

During the week
Try to recognise when you clench your teeth and screw up your face when you are driving, working or resting. Check this also just before you sleep. Notice the way you hold your head and avoid faulty tension in your neck.

The Third Week

Hands and Arms

Look around at any group of men and women and you will see some who betray their inner tensions by holding their arms tight to their sides and gripping their hands so that the knuckles are white – they are almost literally holding themselves in. If you voluntarily relax your hands and arms you will find it a great help to calming down.

Start by shaking one hand as if you were shaking water off it. Then do the same with the other one until the fingers and wrist are loose and relaxed.

Put your hands on your lap and grip them firmly. Recognise this as something you probably do without realising it. Then let the tension go. You will find that you are more likely to relax them if you place one hand cradled in the other with palms either facing upwards or towards you. This is a good position when you are practising relaxing sitting down.

The next exercise for your arms is easier to do standing up. The object is for you to feel and see what your arms are like when they are loose and relaxed.

Stand with your feet a little apart and let your arms dangle loosely by your side. Shake one hand and let the movement spread up your arm to your shoulder so that the muscles wobble. You may have seen swimmers do this before a race. Do the same with the other arm then both together.

Stand with your feet astride and your arms hanging by your side. Turn the top of your trunk so that your shoulders face first one wall then the other without moving

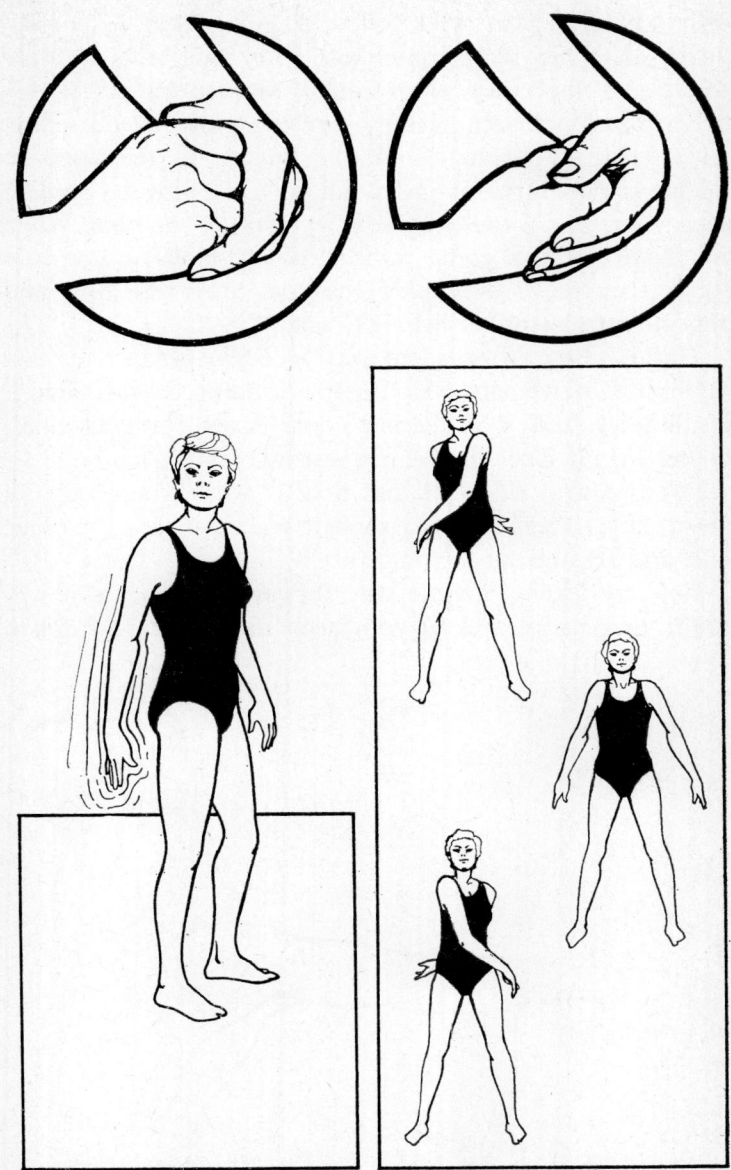

your feet. Let your arms follow round loosely as you do this so that they wrap round you. They should be so loose and heavy that they wrap round because your trunk is twisting and not because they take any part and put themselves there. Your hands hit the outside of the opposite thighs as you turn. In order not to feel giddy be sure to keep your head *looking straight in front all the time*. When you have got this going rhythmically you will know it is correct because it *feels* good and your arms feel loose and almost as if they didn't belong to you.

This is often an excellent way to begin practice. It is a rhythmical movement which helps 'winding down'. Give it a good try, but if it doesn't come easily for you, don't bother with it. Try the next one instead.

Lift one arm sideways and hold it while you recognise the tension. Then let it go so that your arm flops to your side, and breathe out as you do so.

Now try leaning a little way forward (not far or it will strain your back), and let your arms dangle straight down.

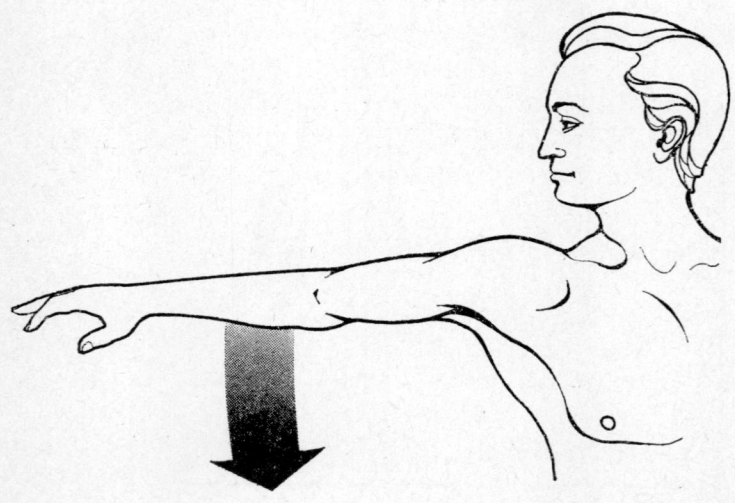

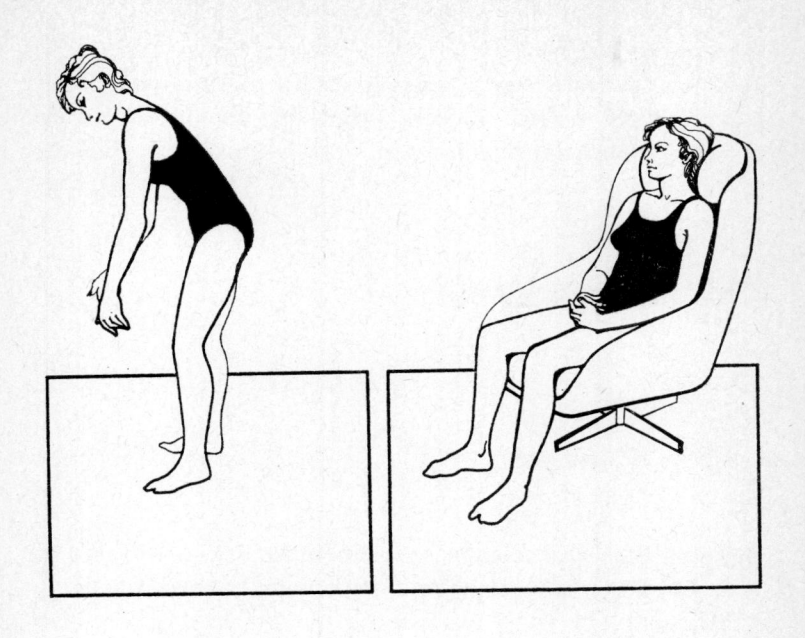

Sway your trunk a little and let your arms swing of their own accord until they come to a standstill. When they are relaxed they feel heavy and as if your hands were a dead weight. If you have a partner to help by giving your arm a little push it should move without any effort from you.

Now combine the earlier exercises:

Sit well supported on your chair, your feet resting on the ground just underneath your knees and support your hands on your lap with one resting on top of the other with the palms facing towards you. Take a few easy calm breaths and think about relaxing your hands, arms, shoulders. Relax your face and jaw and close your eyes softly. After a few minutes you will find that even this short spell of relaxation gives a feeling of calm, and the churning dies down.

During the week
Notice any unnecessary tension in your hands and arms and relax them when you are sitting or walking. Check up on any unnecessary tension in your arms when you are driving and at work.

The Fourth Week

Legs and Ankles

Business men and women are sometimes afraid to relax in case they lose their punch and drive, but the reverse is true. It can enable you to work more quickly and accomplish more in the time with less effort. You may notice that people in high-powered jobs often hold their legs tightly at committee meetings and bend an ankle up strongly with irritation or when faced with a difficult decision. Some people screw up their toes instead, and I know a little boy who wears out his socks under his toes by doing this whenever he has sums for homework or at school. There is no harm at all in these 'displacement' actions when they are brief and ease a situation, but when there is continued tension it adds to fatigue and feelings of strain. Typists who may be sensible about working with shoulders relaxed may be unaware of holding the very large muscles of the legs in day-long contraction.

To relax ankles
Take off your shoes and sit with one leg crossed over the

other. Bend your ankle up towards you strongly and then let it go loose. See if you can shake this ankle loose, then do the same with the other.

To recognise tension in thigh muscles

You can evaluate the degree of tension in the large muscles of the thighs in this way: Sit with the palms of your hands resting on the top of your legs. Begin to straighten one leg but don't actually do it and feel the muscle contract and go tight under your hand. It will do this with only a very little effort on your part and you may well be working like this all day without realising it. Now let the muscles relax and feel the difference. Hold on to the top of your thigh and shake it so that the muscles wobble and feel soft and relaxed. This is another relaxation technique you will see swimmers and athletes using.

Squeeze your legs together, recognise the tension and then let go.

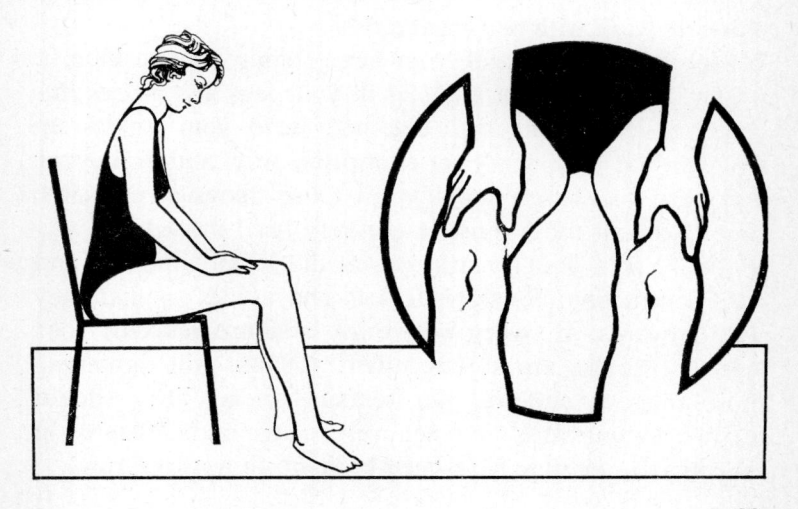

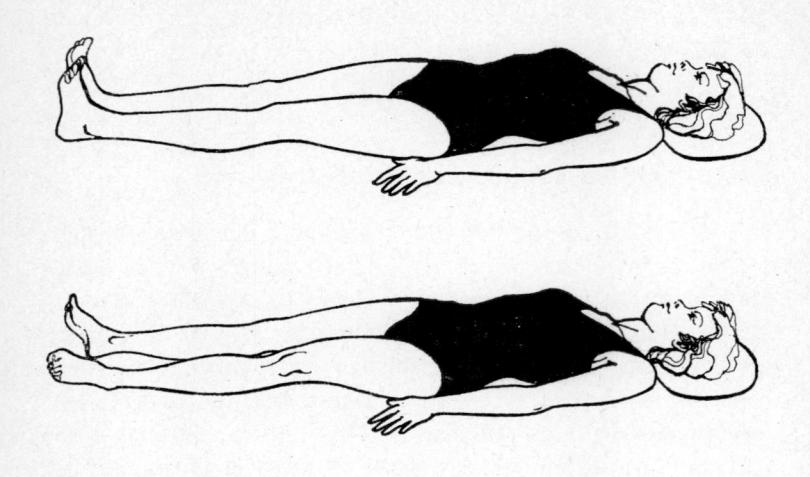

You can do the next exercise better if you lie on the ground, but you can do it on a chair if you really prefer. In this case work with one leg at a time.

Lie on your back with your head resting on a cushion or pillow. Tighten all the muscles in your legs and ankles this way: Squeeze your legs together, bend your ankles up towards you (you won't get cramp this way) and press your legs hard on the ground. Do all those things at the same time. Now all those muscles are very hard indeed and you probably held your breath as you did it. Breathe out and stop contracting. Relax your legs and ankles so that they roll outwards. If, when you think you are relaxed, your legs and ankles are still together, you are still tightening those muscles and are *not* relaxing them. They should easily roll outwards. Women very often find difficulty in relaxing legs as they have been brought up not to sprawl.

During the week
Try to notice when your legs and ankles are held unnecessarily tight. Relax them at committee meetings, when you are typing or sitting, and when you are driving relax them partially at traffic lights and delays. When you come in tired after shopping, rest for a while with your legs up if you find that comfortable. But that isn't sufficient on its own. You must deliberately relax as well.

You are now ready to combine all the previous exercises and in addition practise the deep relaxation shown in the next chapter.

3 Full Relaxation

Someone is sure to say: 'I can relax my body but it is impossible to relax my mind', or: 'I don't need to relax. I can drop off to sleep anywhere.'

Now sleep is not the same thing as relaxation, for it is quite possible to sleep with your fists clenched, your jaw held tight and grinding your teeth. You can be working hard all night while you sleep, so no wonder you wake tired. So although relaxation can be used as an aid to peaceful sleeping it is not the same as dropping off.

There is a close interwoven relationship between body and mind (so much so that perhaps we should not speak of them as separate), and thought is always accompanied by some degree of muscle tension. So if your mind is busy and active, your muscles are *not* relaxed. When there is complete muscle relaxation which you produce yourself, strong mental activity dies down and the mind idles pleasantly in a state of relaxed awareness. It is, I know, very difficult to relax when you are in a state of high excitement, but if you can you have become very skilled in the art. There are some people who have feelings of guilt at relaxing even for a short time. Well, you go ahead and enjoy it. You will soon discover how delightful it feels and how refreshed you are afterwards.

As a general rule, full relaxation is best practised lying

on the floor or a firm surface. It is better not to be too comfortable while you are learning because the aim is to concentrate on muscle relaxation and not to sleep at this stage. Some people may, for several reasons, be better doing full relaxation sitting in a chair, and in any case opportunities for lying on the floor are not always available. Make sure that the small of your back is supported and use a firm cushion there if the chair is badly designed.

Full relaxation sitting on a chair

Sit well back so that your thighs are fully supported. Unless you have long legs you may find it comfortable to rest your feet on a footstool. Support your arms on the sides of the chair or rest your hands loosely on your lap.

If you choose to put your legs up on another chair or a higher stool make sure that there is adequate support for the small of your back.

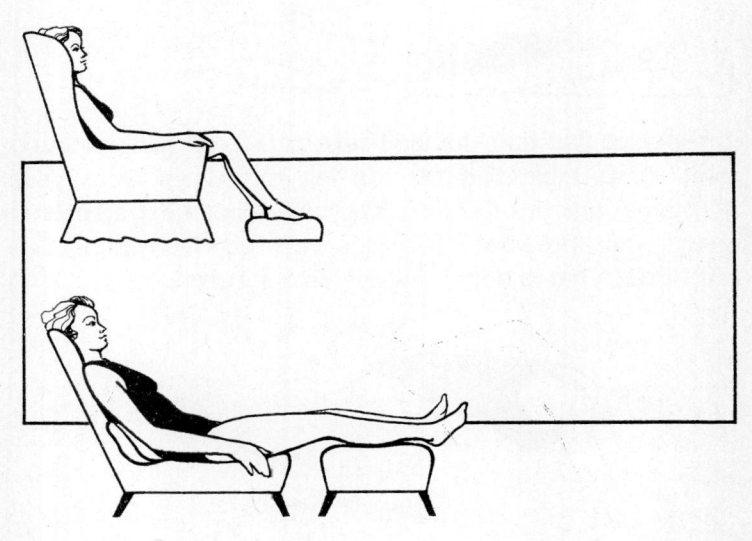

Full relaxation lying on a firm surface
This is probably the best way to learn, but make sure that you are warm and away from draughts.

This is the position with either no head support or using a cushion. Lie with your hands a little away from your sides and your legs just slightly apart so that your limbs are not touching your body.

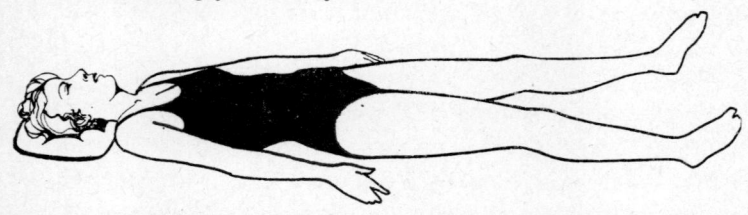

You may find this supported position more comfortable with less strain. Make a wedge shape with pillows under your shoulders and knees so that your abdominal muscles are relaxed. If you are very bony, support your elbows with additional cushions each side.

Many people find this half-side, half-front lying position most comfortable and the top leg tucked up helps your abdominal muscles to relax. You may like an extra cushion under your top knee. This is a very good position on a firm surface but is not so suitable in a soft bed.

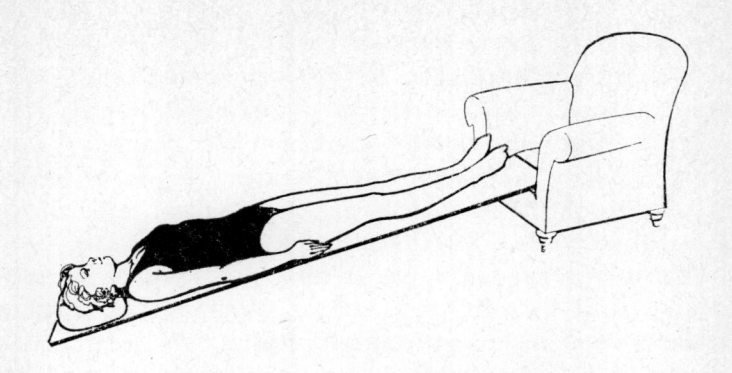

Lying on a slope
If you have varicose veins or piles or have a feeling of downward pressure inside when you have been standing a lot, try lying on a slight slope. Place an ironing board or a plank with the end resting on a *low* divan or chair, or even

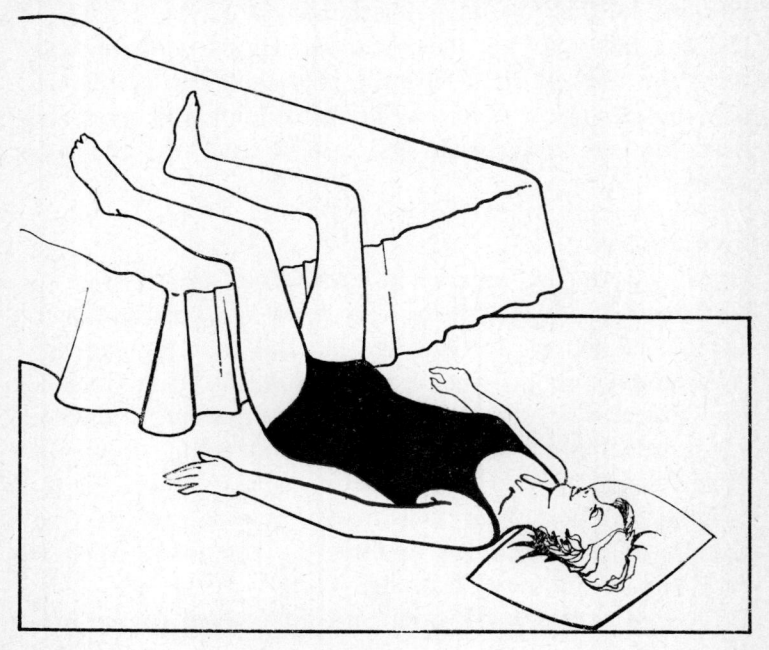

on one or two bricks. Put one or two pillows on the floor to support your head, and rest for ten minutes or so while you deliberately relax. In this way your hips are raised and not just your legs. Don't bother with this position if you have difficulty with breathing. Another way is to lie on your back on the floor with your legs bent at right angles and supported on a low divan or soft chair.

It may be a help when you are first learning to have someone to read these instructions, or you might be able to make a tape recording yourself, reading the instructions slowly in a calm unhurried voice, leaving pauses between each section. Once you have learnt you may find it unnecessary to tighten up muscles to begin. You will just start from where you are and then relax a bit more.

You will discover which is the best order for you to relax muscles and will know which is your own special place for tension. In the following instructions I have begun with relaxing face muscles, then with various parts of the body from the toes up to the head and then finish by relaxing face muscles again. You may prefer to think about relaxing from the toes upwards. In any case, always keep the same order.

Instructions

Before you begin, breathe in and tighten up all over.... Now recognise that as being very tense and breathe out... and let go. Do the same again, but this time, tighten only the amount you do when you are fussed and anxious... recognise this... and let go as you breathe out... then let go a little more than you thought you could, and enjoy this feeling.

Take two or three calm easy breaths, letting your abdominal muscles relax and rise as you do so then go back to your ordinary breathing.

Close your eyes softly and think about each part of your

body in turn . . . let the muscles of your face relax so that your jaw sags a little and make sure that your teeth are not tightly together. Your tongue is shapeless. Relax the muscles of your forehead so that it is smooth and tranquil. Let the expression come off your face. Your neck muscles will relax when your head takes its share of the weight and is resting quite heavily on the pillow.

Now think about your legs. Make sure that your toes are still, and your ankles relaxed . . . let the floor take the whole weight of your legs so that the muscles are soft, and relaxed, and are not working. Let them go . . . and then a little more.

Think about your arms . . . fingers curved, and still, and limp. Your arms are fully supported so that the muscles are soft and relaxed. Now let your shoulders go . . . let the tension go so that you stop contracting.

Now, instead of thinking of yourself in parts, be aware of the whole body relaxing and enjoy the sensation. You can feel your body touching the floor, the muscles relaxed and soft, and no longer working.

And when your muscles are relaxed you feel peaceful . . . and comfortable . . . and you are really resting.

Now it is quite possible that after a few moments your mind has become busy and active again. So check up to find where your muscles have contracted again . . . face . . . toes . . . ankles . . . legs . . . tummy . . . fingers . . . arms . . . shoulders . . . neck . . . face . . . then the all-over sensation . . . now enjoy the sensation of tranquillity and calm when your muscles are relaxed.

In this state of complete relaxation of the muscles under your control, the mind no longer deals with problems but idles effortlessly and creatively, and when the session is over you will feel refreshed and alert. If you need sleep because you have had short nights, don't hesitate to follow relaxation with a daytime nap if you can. You will sleep much better at night if you have released tension in this way during the day.

After relaxing, get up slowly so that you do not feel giddy. You will find that you gradually become able to relax more quickly and for longer spells. At first it may only be for half a minute that you are able to let go, but practice will improve this and as you get more skilled you benefit from the increased composure and refreshed alertness it brings.

If you drop off to sleep during practice

If you are the sort of person who drops off to sleep the minute you start to practise, you will be missing out on the real learning of muscle control. It sometimes helps if you lie with your forearm supported and one hand up. If you drop off, your arm will fall and wake you up.

4 How a Partner Can Help

Although it is quite possible to learn on your own, it is very much easier if you can learn in a small group or with a partner. In our series of classes we always include one session when friends and relatives are invited to attend to learn how they can help their partners, and we have found this most valuable.

One of the problems of learning muscle control is knowing whether or not you have succeeded in recognising degrees of tension and relaxation, of contraction and decontraction. One of the best ways of doing this is to test someone else, and evaluate the varying degrees of relaxation, and you will find that this differs very much from one person to another. There are on the market certain machines that help to illustrate this: electro-myographs, and skin-resistance galvonometers, but although these can be very useful I have found that there is a very special advantage in working with another person. It seems to produce the sympathetic rapport and learning help that no machine could emulate.

So testing and evaluating muscle tension is one way of helping.

Another way is by relieving aching and tension by giving massage to shoulders, neck and forehead. This soothing massage given by someone else feels delightful, can have a marked effect on general relaxation and tranquillity, and will often relieve headaches. There are just a few people who dislike being touched. This is very rare but if it is the case, don't bother with it.

This massage is more than a kindly soothing gesture, for there is a sound scientific basis for its use. The firm massage of shoulders and neck helps the circulation in muscles which may have been in a state of prolonged contraction, and alleviates the aching. In addition, according to the physiologists, the pleasurable stroking has an effect on the hypothalamus, the part of the brain primarily concerned with emotions and stress.

So massage of this kind will help to reduce tension, and then later you can produce this feeling without help. I have included the kind of massage that can be done anywhere and doesn't require getting undressed, although it is more effective on bare skin.

If you are helping someone else, these points may be useful: Begin by feeling as calm as possible yourself and you will communicate this to your partner. It will show in your relaxed movements and gestures, your facial expression and especially in your voice. Speak in a calm unhurried way, pitch your voice a little lower and have slightly longer pauses than usual. Although you need quiet authority, don't be too brisk or hectoring and try not to be very concerned about success for it takes time. If you say: 'No, that's hopeless. You're as stiff as a board', you are unlikely to succeed in helping. You will increase anxiety and feelings of inadequacy and make matters worse. Instead, build on every tiny success. If, for example, you find that wrist and fingers are relaxed, say so at once, and build on from there. Taught in this way everyone improves, even if it is only a little, and your quiet approval will act as reinforcement for future learning. Remember that it takes time to change old habits, so don't hurry.

It is not much help asking your partner to make the

mind a blank, or to conjure up visual images such as fields of daffodils or black velvet. When you are really relaxed you do not deliberately make these images. As your muscles let go their tensions, after a while it may be that spontaneous visual images drift gently across your relaxed awareness with no conscious effort on your part. We are concerned with discovering the pleasure of feeling relaxed through muscle control, and to use this skill not to withdraw from the world but to make it a part of daily living.

Another way of helping is to encourage regular practice. You may well be the first to recognise the mounting tension, and as we are concerned with the preventative aspect of these techniques, this is the time to help.

Testing relaxation of arms
Put one hand under your partner's elbow and one hand under her wrist. Move the arm gently, and if it is relaxed it will feel heavy and limp and your partner takes no part in the movement. Feel the difference when your partner deliberately tightens her muscles and holds her arm in position by her own effort. Get her to relax her arm again, probably she will do this better with her eyes closed and she should not talk to you. This can be done sitting, standing or lying down.

Your partner leans forward just a little so that her arms dangle loosely. Give one arm a gentle push so that it swings like a pendulum without your partner doing anything.

Testing relaxation of shoulders
Stand behind your partner and rest your hands lightly on top of the shoulders. Ask her to tighten up a little and feel how the muscles have become hard. Ask her to relax

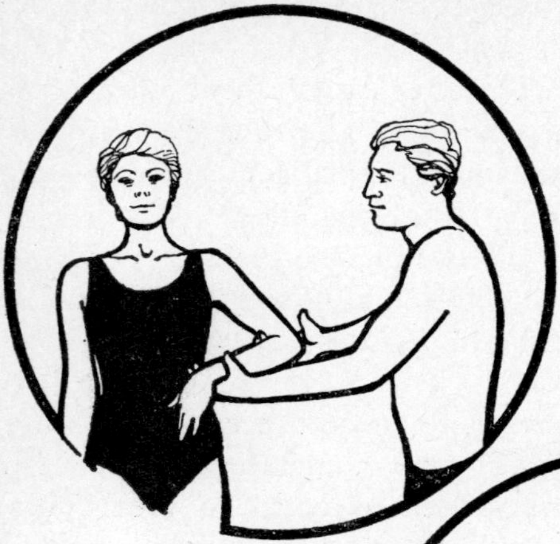

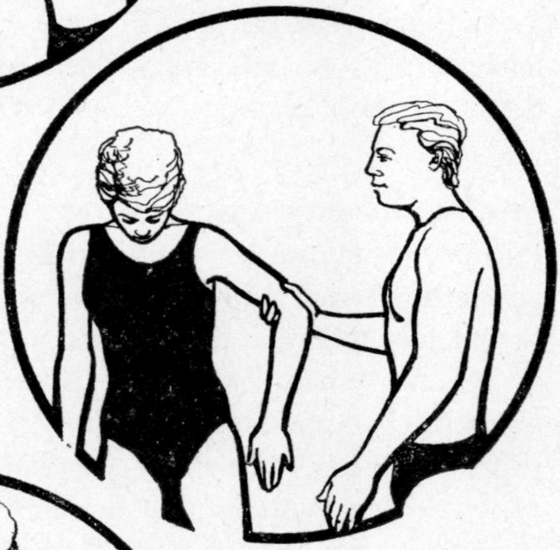

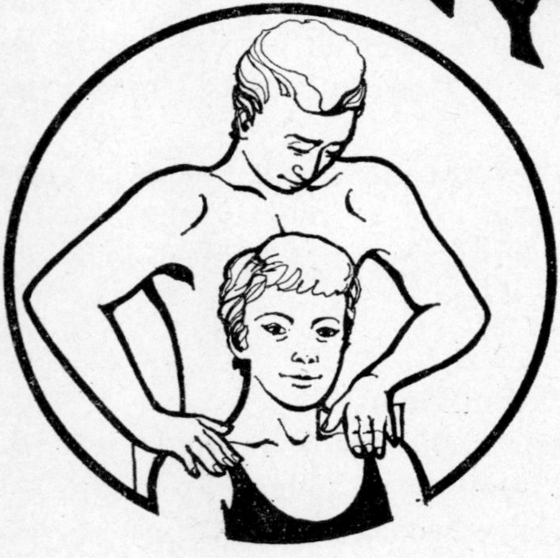

and then feel the difference. Do the same with your hands on the top of the arms near the shoulders.

Massage of shoulders
Place your hands lightly on top of the shoulders and ask your partner to relax them. Reach down with your thumbs, keeping your fingers where they are and firmly roll the skin upwards towards the top of the shoulders each side of the spine. Do this with the amount of pressure your partner finds most comfortable. Make circular movements with the fleshy part of your thumb or fingers where your partner indicates she is particularly tense. Smoothe only the fleshy part, not the bone, and don't dig your fingers in.

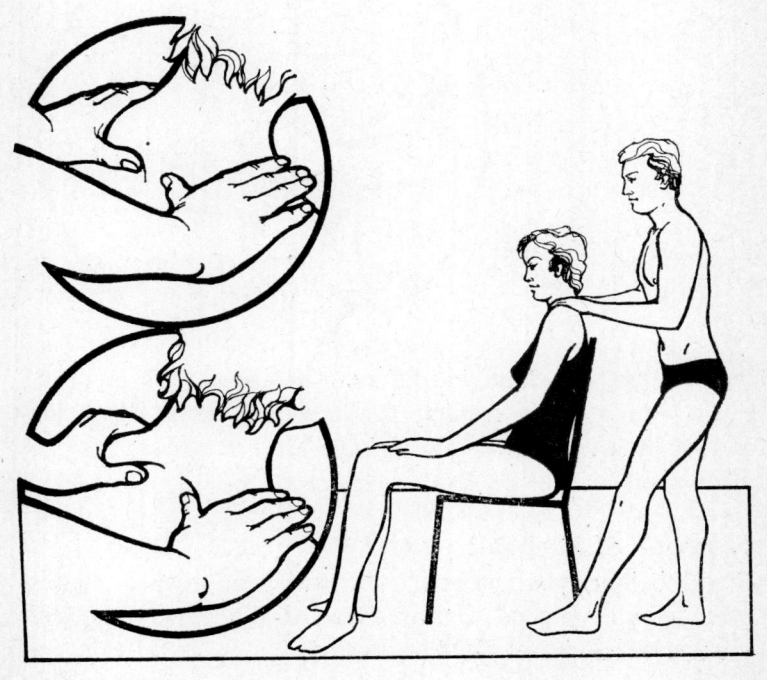

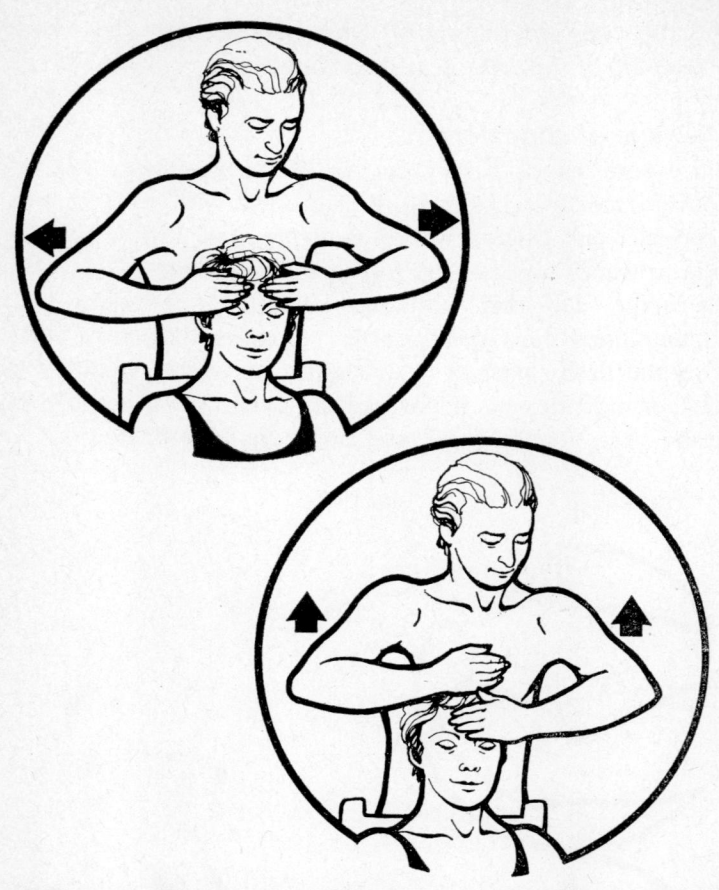

This can be done in different positions, for example, sitting on a chair leaning forward with your head supported by a cushion. You can include some massage for the neck also.

Massage of forehead
Stand behind your partner with her head resting against you. You may need to lean forward a little so that your partner's head is not tilted backwards.

Tell your partner to close the eyes softly and relax shoulders, hands and arms. Smooth your fingers gently from the middle out towards the temples. Do this for a while then change to moving each hand alternately upwards towards the hairline.

When a partner's help is specially needed

Although this book is primarily concerned with muscle control, it is important to have an idea of some of our basic emotional needs. These are common to everybody and if they are not met the result can be tension and unhappiness. But I know that when those around have some understanding of these needs and can give support when they are inevitably threatened from time to time, it can make all the difference between going under and keeping balance. Some of these basic emotional needs are described below.

We need security
This will mean different things to different people, but we know that any sudden change in life patterns will give rise to some stress and anxiety. This will be the case whether the upheavals are tragic or unpleasant such as bereavement, separation, redundancy or even retirement, or exciting such as marriage, change of house or job, or even, for some vulnerable people, holidays.

We need to give and receive affection
'Affection' means more than the popular interpretation of the word. It means our desire to belong and to be accepted for what we are by those we care about. To be excluded, to feel abandoned and lonely creates anxiety. We also want to give affection and to feel that this is accepted by others. Unfortunately it is when people are most unlikeable that

they are in most need of affection, and may also feel unable to give it in case it is rejected.

We need recognition and self-esteem

We all have a desire for a sense of our personal worth. We need our quota of self-esteem and recognition of our special abilities whether it is at home, at work or with our friends. We can feel humiliated by a work experience when mistakes have been made, or by social bloomers. At home a mother can easily lose her self-esteem when an adolescent belittles her appearance, her house, cooking or behaviour. Some people are more easily thrown off balance than others and are very hurt by criticism.

We need new experiences and responsibilities

This may appear to conflict with the need for security, but as one psychologist has put it: 'Man desires both the fat of security and the pepper of insecurity'. Over-security can be stifling, and we need to accept challenge and responsibility without someone breathing down our necks all the time. Tackling new skills, undertaking new experiences can, if they are within our ability, bring exhilaration and a sense of well-being.

We need creative leisure or work activities

Just as children discharge their emotions through play so adults need to have the kind of leisure pursuits which give them satisfaction. A few people have vitally interesting and creative jobs, but most will need some opportunities to develop what abilities they have in a creative manner, to 'do their own thing'. It may be a hobby or making a home or garden, or it may be painting or music or taking part in a sport. Whatever it is, there is a recharging of batteries, a re-creation and a release from day-to-day tension. We need to make spaces in our leisure time for some absorbing occupation.

It is inevitable that at times these needs cannot be met and there will be resulting anxiety and tension. When this goes on for a long time the result will show itself in the physical disorders mentioned earlier. But a sympathetic relative, friend or colleague can help in several ways. Most people can cope with the loss of one of these emotional satisfactions in one area of life if it is made up in another. For example, if self-esteem has been damaged at work perhaps with promotion passing by, or by a humiliating brush with colleagues, it can perhaps be made up at home in some way, or success at leisure pursuits may bring encouragement and self-esteem in this area.

An observant, sympathetic partner can be aware of these times when help is especially needed, and some understanding of the way we all have these basic emotional needs will help. It will mean accepting some letting-off of steam as a safety valve without getting too involved, and it will also be the time to encourage relaxation practice before the pressures get too great.

The final thing to remember is that we all have our breaking point and if medical assistance is necessary the partner can help with the acceptance of this and support treatment. However it has been shown that when relaxation techniques have been practised in time and made part of daily living, there is a marked decrease in the need for tranquillisers and sedatives.

5 Pre-menstrual Tension and the Menopause

This chapter is not only for women. It is intended also for men who may be baffled and exasperated by the fluctuating moods of women who are experiencing the symptoms of pre-menstrual tension or who are going through the menopause.

I have heard women say about their pre-menstrual behaviour: 'If only he'd understand that I'm *not* really like that.' 'The children must think I'm an awful mother when I yell at them. I wish they understood.' 'I sometimes think I must be going round the bend, or else that my husband thinks that I am.'

There is no time in a woman's life when she is not subject to the ebb and flow of the hormones that control the menstrual cycle. All women experience physiological changes, but most can manage without any disruption of their daily life. There are, however, some women who herald their menstrual periods with several days of irrational irritability, depression or lethargy and some have additional symptoms such as water retention which leads to a temporary gain in weight, headaches and a tendency to become accident prone and clumsy. All this usually occurs a few days before the periods begin.

It is important to realise that this has a well-recognised physical cause even though the full reasons are not yet fully understood, and is not just neurotic behaviour.

The changes which occur during the menstrual cycle are initiated by the hypothalamus, the part of the brain which is closely connected with our emotions. It is not difficult to understand that this may account for the occasions familiar to many women when shock, excitement or change can upset the menstrual clock and delay the onset of menstruation, bring it on earlier or even stop it for quite a long time. It can effect emotional feelings too.

Every twenty-eight days or so (and the *or so* is significant for there is a very wide and normal variation), the wall of the uterus grows a thick spongy lining rich in blood vessels to prepare it for the implanting of the egg released from one of the ovaries at this time. The breasts begin to prepare for lactating and other changes occur. If the egg is not fertilised the lining strips away and is discharged along with the egg cell as the menstrual flow. Then the cycle starts all over again.

All these changes are regulated by the intricate interactions between two of the hormones of the pituitary gland, and the two hormones manufactured by the ovaries, oestrogen and progesterone. The word 'hormone' comes from the Greek and means 'to stir up' and this is an apt description of their action. Each of the four hormones in its turn is released, initiates one step in the procedure, paves the way for the next hormone, and then makes its exit. All the endocrine glands in the body are interrelated and any disturbance in one of them can affect the others. Under stress, the adrenal glands may over-react as part of the Fight or Flight mechanism and this will contribute to some of the symptoms of pre-menstrual tension as will any imbalance of oestrogen and progesterone.

If the symptoms are serious medical assistance will be necessary, but relaxation techniques have been found to help many women at these times. It will mean attention to the calming-down practice even though this is a time when women may feel disinclined to do so, and understanding and support from the family. Anxiety and tension are very catching so it is important for those around not to get swept up in the mounting tension themselves. If the periods are regular and predictable it will be helpful to plan for a quieter programme for a few days before menstruation begins.

The Menopause

It is curiously human and relatively modern to have a menopause. It is unknown amongst mammals in the wild, and in short-lived primitive societies it was very rare for a woman to live on after her childbearing days had finished. Today she is likely to have a quarter of a century after her menstrual periods have ceased in which to enjoy a new way of living: a change of life.

The word menopause comes from the Greek meaning *cessation* of the monthly flow, not a *pause* at all. It was once considered that at every seven years of life there were bodily changes that marked a new step up the ladder of life. Infancy ended at seven years, puberty was reached at fourteen, adulthood at twenty one, the menopause at forty two and the life span ended at seventy (though few reached this age). Today of course these figures no longer apply: puberty begins earlier, the menopause later and the expectation of life, especially for women is considerably longer.

Somewhere between the ages of 45 to 55 a woman's ovaries gradually stop producing mature eggs, grow smaller, and cease to produce their special hormones. To compensate for the change in chemical output, extra work is thrown on other endocrine glands, especially the adrenals. It takes time for these to adapt to the change and sometimes they produce too much, sometimes too little, but eventually a balance is reached. It is this temporary imbalance which causes most of the disturbances some women experience at the menopause.

About 15 per cent of women have little or no trouble at all, but others may experience a variety of symptoms which are usually harmless but which can be puzzling and frightening if their cause and temporary nature is not understood. There is much needless ignorance and superstition surrounding the menopause, and anxiety about it can affect all members of the household. When mother's health and balance is upset it will influence the emotional wellbeing of all the family. This is why it is important that the menfolk and older children should have some understanding of its effects. It really can make all the difference to a woman coping with disturbances of chemical balance if those closely connected with her can give sympathetic and practical support. They can all be confident that adjustment will ultimately be reached by almost every woman.

For the lucky ones whose bodies adapt easily and gradually, the menstrual periods get less and less with longer intervals between them until they cease. Hardly any other changes are noticeable.

Other women will experience some symptoms in varying degrees, and the most common of these are hot flushes and sweating. These can be slight and transient, or severe enough to warrant medical aid, and they can occur months or even years before the periods begin to alter. They are caused by the occasional erratic functioning of the nerve mechanisms which normally keep the calibre of the blood vessels in close check. They can either be quite unpredictable or they may be sparked off by slight awkwardness or embarrassment.

The accompanying sensations vary greatly. They may begin with a curious feeling of dread and doom experienced in the pit of the stomach (and once you know that this has a physical cause you can accept that it is not just a state of mind). Sometimes there is nasal congestion or there may be feelings of general tension. Then waves of heat spread over the upper part of the body, especially the face and neck. Although the woman herself may feel that everyone must be noticing it, a glance in the mirror will assure her that very little is apparent. She may hurry to open the window saying that the room is too hot, then ten minutes later, when she is at the sweating stage, will close it again because she feels cold. After the flush has died away there is a feeling of relaxation again. Several women have remarked that during a cold winter they welcomed their flushes . . . the only time they felt really warm, they said.

Since the flushes give an indication of the measure of glandular imbalance, it is not surprising if the woman does not feel at her best at this time. If the symptoms are severe, and sweating so profuse that sleep is disturbed, she should not hesitate to seek medical advice, for there are drugs which may help her. In the end however the body must come to terms with it and will adjust to the change.

Another circulatory disturbance which may occur at this time is the occasional giddy attack which arrives in a swirl out of the blue. It's no joke to find the room spinning uncontrollably round you without warning. If the medical check-up reveals nothing organically wrong, just accept it and be interested in the proceedings. Chalk it up to experience and wait for it to move off.

Equally surprising are the sudden blanks of memory, especially for recent events. It can be embarrassing when you forget the name of someone you knew well half an hour ago, and irritating for those around when things are mislaid. If you are normally a scatty feckless creature, you can take this in your careless stride, but it is humiliating for a competent orderly woman to have this kind of upset.

Fatigue is another very common symptom. It's not the ordinary tiredness and exhaustion that most men and women experience at times, but waves of overwhelming fatigue without any obvious cause. This needs recognition and understanding and a planned programme of relaxation and rest, with support for this by those around. Those who are troubled by this form of fatigue should read Dr Marion Hilliars's book *Women and Fatigue* for it gives warm understanding and practical advice on how to cope.

I have heard women at the menopause say: 'I can't understand it. She's over sixty and she has far more energy than I have.' Well, so she should. She has reached a state of equilibrium in her hormonal balance and is enjoying renewed vigour now that the menopause is over.

Many women find that their normal emotions are exaggerated at this time and this has its effect on those around. 'Tell me, Mum,' said a teenage boy, 'what on earth makes a woman tick? I never know what to expect.' Indeed, Mum herself may find her moods unpredictable and feel guilty about her outbursts. It would often be helpful if older children understood a little about the mood swings of women at times of hormonal imbalance for they are not unlike those experienced at adolescence. It is just bad luck if mother is at the menopause at the time when her childern are passing through adolescence, especially as this may coincide with the need to care for ageing parents.

These heightened emotions may cause outbursts of irrational irritability, or there may be feelings of gloom and despair. She may burst into tears for trivial reasons and may be profoundly moved by plays and books. One woman said that she had not been able to attend her son's school carol concerts for two years because she found the music so moving that she sobbed. This was someone who is normally very composed and when the menopause was over she returned to her usual self.

Sometimes there are feelings of inadequacy and lack of confidence, with increased sensitivity to criticism. This may be particularly so of business and professional women who can be assured that this is a passing phase and no one need notice.

This heightened emotional intensity can have its uses. There may be a surge of creativity and an exquisite awareness of beauty with an increased sensitivity to everything around. This can be an enriching and rewarding experience to be cherished and put to good use.

It is not surprising if these emotional reactions produce an increase in tension headaches, and women who suffer in this way will benefit from relaxation techniques.

Since hormones are closely concerned with the digestive processes the temporary imbalance may be responsible for the rumbling flatulence that some women experience, though a medical check-up is sensible.

How others can help

Many women pass through the change of life with cheerful disregard of their upsets, but it is unkind and unhelpful to dismiss the more serious disturbances as negligible or amusing. They are the result of real chemical changes in the body and it is *not* all in the mind.

Those around can help considerably to make the change a smoother one. We have already seen how closely the action of the glands is linked with emotions, and anything which can give a feeling of calm will help the functioning. Tolerant, good-humoured understanding by those at home and work will be a great help at this time.

No one should be too hurt or troubled by a woman's moods; they are probably as unpredictable to her as to anyone else and she will be full of remorse when they are over, even if she won't show it. It is when everyone around joins in the fray that the situation gets red hot and unmanageable.

Fatigue at the menopause should be recognised for what it is and ways should be devised to deal with it. A willingness by the family to take over some of the chores for the time being and an insistence that rest periods are observed will help to remove some of her feelings of guilt and inadequacy. But this needs to be done cheerfully *before* she feels that she cannot give up. Some women get to the state of fatigue and tension when they appear to wallow in self-martyrdom and cannot relinquish their duties and may even take on more and more. Be firm about it, take over what you can, encourage relaxation practice and relieve her anxiety at letting the house go a bit. A lively rested mother is worth more to her family's well-being than a spotless kitchen floor.

The woman at work may need to delegate some of her duties for a while, to drop some of the inessential jobs and accept temporary setbacks without fuss. Her friends can help by understanding that she may be better if she cuts down her late night social commitments for a while and has more rest and relaxation.

How the Woman Can Help Herself

If you are approaching the menopause you will find that by understanding the nature of the changes that are happening you can avoid the panic which increases tension. If you are worried by unusual symptoms it is of course sensible to visit your doctor but it is likely that you are experiencing the sensations that women all over the world have in varying degrees. They may last only months or may spread over several years with diminishing severity.

Many women who have learnt how to relax agree that it has helped them at this time. If you can get a group together to practise it is much easier. When several of you are in the same boat you will find that the exercises are lighthearted fun as well as being helpful, and the massage is soothing and helps relaxation.

In addition to this, you will relieve much of the tension and fatigue if you incorporate muscle relaxation into everyday life, recognising any unnecessary tension and releasing it. Then put aside daily periods for full relaxation and rest, and be firm about planning this. Let the chores go for a while, and if your sleep has been disturbed at night catch up with a daytime sleep. Begin with deliberate relaxation then enjoy a guilt-free sleep for a while... and be blowed to what the neighbours think. If you have a relaxed sleep you will awake feeling silky-smooth and rested, and you are more likely to sleep better at night if the tension has been released in this way.

Try also to snatch odd moments of relaxation during the day, even if it is only for three minutes or so, and you will find that you can control the mounting tension and feelings will calm down. Don't wait until you are exhausted and tense, but make it part of your living pattern. Try speaking a little more slowly and pitch your voice slightly lower, for it helps those around you to simmer down when you speak calmly.

Don't waste time and energy feeling guilty and miserable if you have let fly on one of your bad days. Accept it as temporary, hope that the family understands and make it up to them on your good days. It will pass. Most emotions can be influenced by glands, and most glands are influenced by emotions. By learning and applying relaxation techniques you are on the way to exerting some control over these states. You will soon learn how much stress you can accommodate and plan accordingly. One woman who was at the menopause was having to care for difficult old people as well as her older children and she found her tension was getting unmanageable. She deliberately put into practice all she had learnt about relaxation and said that although her problems remained the same she could avoid letting them affect her physically, and in this way found she could cope.

Women who have had a hysterectomy operation (the removal of the womb) may be surprised to find that even though they have had no menstrual periods since the operation they may still have the symptoms of the menopause at the appropriate time. This is because wherever possible the surgeon will leave the ovaries intact so that there is no abrupt change of hormonal level and the menopause is gradual.

Some doctors say that the menopause is too often used as an excuse to explain away various physical and psychological disorders, and the less said about it the better. This may sometimes be true, and some women do appear to exploit their menopausal symptoms. However, it is also the lack of information, and the fear born of ignorance and old wives' tales that increases tension and magnifies symptoms. The Family Doctor booklet *The Change of Life*, published by the BMA, is a helpful and authoritative guide.

From all this it might appear that the woman is the only one under pressure at this stage of life. Although the man does not have a menopause in the same way as a woman, this is often the time in his life when he is under great stress and has additional anxieties at home and work. 'He's work mad,' said one wife, 'he's addicted to it and never lets up.' Women should try to understand the pressures at this middle-age period and do all they can to encourage relaxation to relieve the tension and stress which can be particularly damaging to health at this time.

6 Putting it into practice

If you want to alter a habit of muscle tension which you may have acquired over a lifetime it will take time and practice. So go slowly. Relaxation is ease. But because the learning is incorporated into daily living it does not require long spells of practice, and once you have learnt the skill you will only use the preliminary exercises on special occasions.

Don't be surprised at first if you begin to wonder whether the whole thing isn't becoming an obsession, that you think about it all the time and fear that you'll be looking for tension in your muscles for the rest of your life. This is all part of the initial learning process and it will pass. Imagine you are learning to write fluently with your left hand when you are normally right-handed. At first you deliberately practise and think about it a lot because you reach a stage when you seem to make no progress and you feel it's hopeless. This is a plateau of learning. But if you stick at it, gradually, almost without realising it, you find you are no longer thinking about it, you have acquired the skill and it has become part and parcel of you for ever.

During the learning stage, set aside two periods in the day when you can practise. I have found that it is more realistic to suggest only ten to fifteen minutes practice at a time because almost everyone can manage that somehow and it is quite adequate for learning. Choose the time of day that suits you best but don't wait until you are really tired. Give the exercises I have suggested a good try, but if they don't suit you, don't bother. The others will do. Get someone to help you by testing muscle tension and giving massage to shoulders and forehead if you like it. After doing the preliminary exercises go on to full relaxation, on the floor if you can, for it is easier to learn on a firm surface with your whole body supported. Later on, anywhere will do. After a while you will not need to tighten up your muscles before you relax them. You will start from where you are and go on from there to relax further and further.

At first, have very short spells of full relaxation and stop as soon as your mind is active and muscles tense. Check up and try again. You may achieve relaxation only for a few seconds to begin with, but later on you will reach the delicious stage of gentle drifting when your mind idles without conscious effort and cuts off from its problems.

Some Don'ts for Beginners

Don't think you should be doing something else. When you have settled down to relax you may begin to think of all the other things you should be doing. Relaxation will mean time saved in the end so don't feel guilty about it. One woman who felt like this plays a long play record so softly that she doesn't have to listen to it and she is content to relax until it ends. It times practice for her in a way she enjoys.

Don't try to relax. Just stop contracting muscle.

Don't think you can only relax when you are lying down.

This idea has put many people off practising. Although deep relaxation is best achieved in this way, you can practise it quite well on a bus, sitting on a chair or partially as you work.

Don't go to sleep while you are practising. Save it for afterwards.

Don't try to make your mind a blank. You can't. When you want to calm down, breathe easily and do whatever it is you do when you relax your muscles. There are other ways, but try this first.

Don't think that watching television, knitting or playing golf counts as relaxation practice. It may be recreation but you can be quite tense doing it.

Don't think you can make up at night for the rest you needed in the day, and don't build up a sleep debt which will be difficult to repay.

Don't be afraid of telling people you need to relax. One tired woman who had friends staying with her at Christmas was apprehensive about this. Eventually in the afternoon she said: 'I'm sorry but I'm off to relax for half an hour'. She discovered how delighted her guests were to have the opportunity for a rest too, and they all felt refreshed afterwards.

7 Relaxation for Living

Once you have learnt to relax you may be able to incorporate it into daily living without setting aside a special time for practice. Some people, though, are better with a planned daily period of exercises as well as full relaxation, and many will find that at times of stress they must take time out to regain inner quiet. So your practice must be planned to meet your individual needs and no single scheme will suit everyone. The suggestions that follow are based on the experiences of many men and women I know who have put the techniques into practice.

Driving

Frustration, raised blood pressure and accidents are the tension scourge of the driver in today's traffic conditions. Before you set off give yourself a few seconds – it doesn't take more than this – to quieten down and make a relaxed start. Drive with your hands resting lightly on the wheel and try to notice tension in your shoulders, jaw and forehead. Let your left leg and ankle relax when they are not being used. Use traffic lights and delays as a bonus, taking a few easy calm breaths and making it a practice period. You will find that you are less fatigued and irritable but your alertness remains. After a business deal or an exacting meeting, wait a few moments and calm down with conscious relaxation before you drive off.

If you are a passenger, and suffer from tension headaches or migraine on long journeys, plan well beforehand so that you are not rushed and agitated before you start. Then have as many stops as you conveniently can, and for part of these times, either stay in the car, or rest on the grass, and practise controlled relaxation. We have found that by this deliberate planning many people who dreaded holidays and long journeys have been able to manage successfully.

Housework

You can do some of the exercises while you work and the more rhythmical you can make your movements the less fatigued you are likely to be. Some women found that the relaxed arm swinging, done while they waited for the kettle to boil, gave them a feeling of looseness and ease. Notice how often you grit your teeth when you do unpleasant jobs, and when you hold your jaw tightly. Check up on your shoulders when you do the washing-up and other chores where this kind of tension is unnecessary. Some backache is the result of sustained tension and if this is the case, break off at intervals to have a stretch and twist and take short rest spells sitting with your back well supported by a cushion. But try to do this *before* fatigue sets in. To avoid strain caused by faulty ways of lifting make sure that you keep your back straight as you lift, using bent knees to help you reach down, and hold the object close to your body.

It may be a good plan to break off your morning chores at elevenses time and have your relaxation practice then. One woman who used this time to settle down and relax on a rug on the floor said that at first her dog was surprised but now joins her for the fifteen minutes relaxation period. Others may prefer a spell after lunch or just before the children come home from school. If you have small children the only time available may be when they are having their nap, or you may have to do it when father takes over or after they are in bed.

We mustn't forget the problems of the young father. In these days of sharing he may often help in the house and sometimes get up to care for the baby at night. He may be short of sleep, irritated and fatigued, and in addition has to face demanding work situations. This can be a serious situation and must be tackled sensibly before it mounts to unmanageable proportions. This form of stress differs very much between individuals and according to the circumstances. It comes down to knowing yourself and those you live with, recognising tension and taking action early on without being ashamed of it. Don't wait until you explode.

A working mother has different problems. For some the change of occupation and change of pace is a refreshment in itself, but for others it is an added strain. Relaxation of unnecessary tension during work, good practice periods when travelling on buses or trains and a spell in the lunch break will help. Massage of shoulders, neck and forehead by someone else is a delightful way of being helped to relax and simmer down. One husband helps his wife by massaging her as she sits on a cushion on the floor in front of him and he watches television at the same time. She says that he's prepared to go on much longer in this way! One mother arranges her relaxation period as soon as she comes home. She leaves out a snack for the children, an apple or a sandwich, and they know that she needs to be quiet for fifteen minutes. Still resting, she listens to the day's news and then is ready to prepare the evening meal in a refreshed way. She said this helped her not to bawl at the children as soon as they came in, and they settled down too.

At Work

If you are in a high-powered job you will need to plan your relaxation carefully so that you are able to work with maximum efficiency. You may need to set apart times for undisturbed relaxation periods which are honoured by everybody around. One very successful business man was known by all his staff to have the fifteen minutes after lunch as his relaxation time and no possible crisis was allowed to interfere with it. If you are one of those with stomach upsets of nervous origin, ten minutes relaxation before a meal is a great help to digestion, and you should try never to eat when you are tense. Use relaxation to calm down first. During committee meetings you can relax legs under the table, your hands and arms, and at times take several deliberate calm breaths. Then when your turn comes you can use all your energy and force.

When you get home the family must be helped to understand that you should have a short time for quiet relaxation before the evening meal or before you discuss the day's problems.

If you are a manual worker your fatigue is of a different kind, not caused by your unnecessary tension but by the actual form of your work. Errors of performance and accidents occur during fatigue, so try to make your work as rhythmical and as economical of effort as possible. Look out for excessive muscle tension and try to recognise a build-up of fatigue. It is however those engaged in sedentary occupations with long periods of sustained muscle contraction and conflicting emotional tensions who are most likely to suffer.

Typing, or prolonged working at a desk may cause

aching and stiffness in the shoulders and neck. Check up on tension in these areas and relax those muscles, and make sure that your chair is high enough so that you are not having to raise your shoulders unnecessarily. A cushion may be the answer, and if you have backache, have another firm cushion to support the small of your back. Check up on head and neck posture and avoid slumping.

When you are working under pressure, stop at intervals and relax for a few moments. Shake your wrists, move your head and give some massage to your neck. Then type or write slowly for a sentence or two and you will find that you speed up immediately afterwards. But try to relax *before* you get really fatigued. You'll save time in the end.

One group of office girls who suffered from tension headaches joined up together for relaxation practice in the lunch hour. They did the exercises together, and gave shoulder massage and then sat quietly and relaxed for five minutes before returning to work.

I tell the members of the classes to use every opportunity to practice. One woman who did this at the hairdressers, relaxed under the dryer, face and all. But the assistant thought she was ill and sent for the store's nurse!

One University professor explained how he uses relaxation to heighten his awareness and enhance creative thinking. When he has a difficult lecture to prepare, or research material to assemble, he gathers up all the available information then spends at least an hour in full conscious relaxation. After this he finds he thinks clearly and there is almost a flash of creativity. He can then work with his mind uncluttered and the jigsaw falls into place.

Dealing with pain

Pain itself is exhausting and those who have to live with it know there is no easy answer. Pain can increase muscle tension and this in its turn produces pain. Now this part of it you *can* deal with. The more you can relax the more manageable it becomes and you are not increasing your difficulties.

Some women who have painful menstrual periods have found that if they practise the deep breathing and relaxation recommended for training for childbirth it has helped them with the spasmodic contractions and relieves pain. More information about this can be obtained from the National Childbirth Trust, 9 Queensborough Terrace, London W2.

Insomnia

If you suffer from insomnia you will know better than anyone else how wrong people are when they say it doesn't matter if you go without sleep so long as you are resting. You know quite well that it *does* matter. People who can drop off to sleep anywhere are of a different kind and usually have no idea of the difficulties of the light, easily-disturbed sleeper. You will have discovered also that drugs are not really the answer except for emergencies or to break a habit of not sleeping well.

You really can help yourself out of this horror, though it takes time and practice and above all confidence in your ability. How you sleep at night will depend on how you spend the day, so you need to take this seriously and plan accordingly. At first you will require several relaxation periods in the day and somehow make an opportunity for a daytime sleep as well, after you have done the exercises. The sleep may be a nap after lunch or later in the afternoon or even when you come in from work if you can manage it. You will find that an hour's sleep in the day is worth several tossing at night, especially if it is planned for, and you don't feel guilty at taking it. At night you will be more relaxed and the tension has been broken so that you will sleep more easily. If you do wake in the night, relax again deliberately and calmly without getting angry at the noise that woke you. You will more easily slip off to sleep again this way, and if you *know* that there will be an opportunity to sleep for a while in the day you won't be so frightened. Don't be ashamed of planning this way; eventually the tension will get less and you can take up your usual pattern of life with zest. But you will need to watch the sleep debt. If you have one or two really late nights, make up for it by going to bed early the next, or by having a daytime nap. And for you, of all people, the daily living practice is particularly important and you must know yourself well enough to assess how much excitement you can take at one go without being knocked off balance.

Relaxation is a good commonsense way of dealing with the stresses and strains of our modern life. If we use it wisely we can gain in self-awareness and an understanding of our body-mind integration. This will enable us to work and play to full physical capacity, enhance our relationships with other people and to attain the precious inner quiet and stability we need in a hectic changing world.

8 Quick Reference Guide

Choose the exercises which suit you best. Once you have learnt to recognise tension you will not need this kind of practice but will relax at will, using the exercises only as a help on special occasions. Finish with a spell of full relaxation.

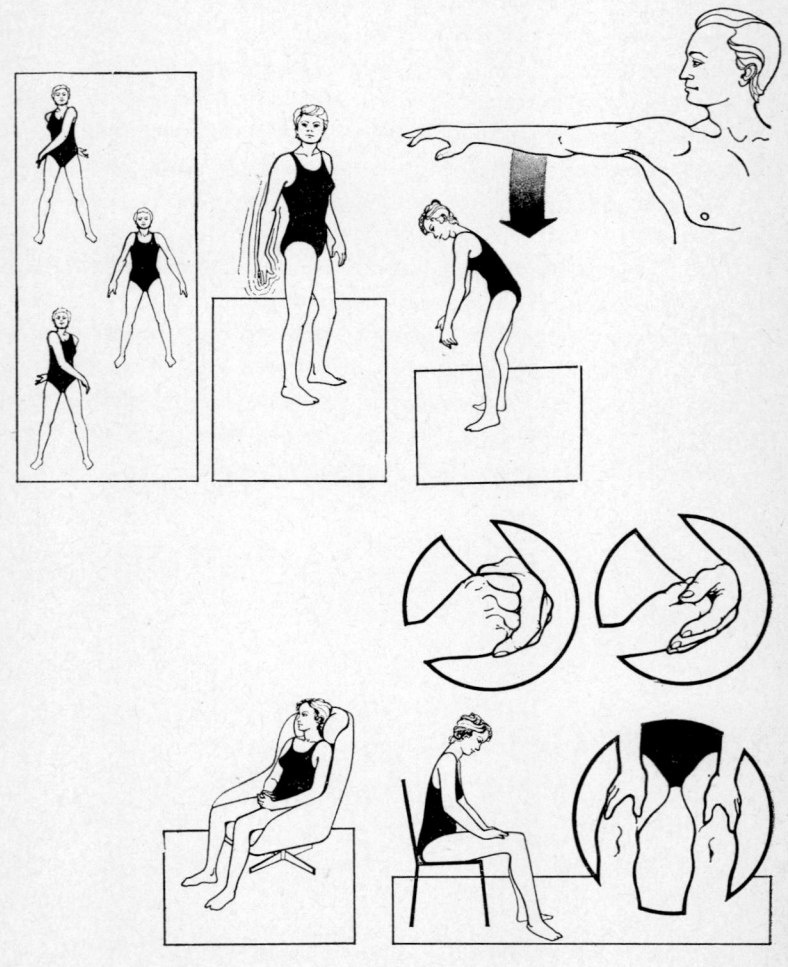

79

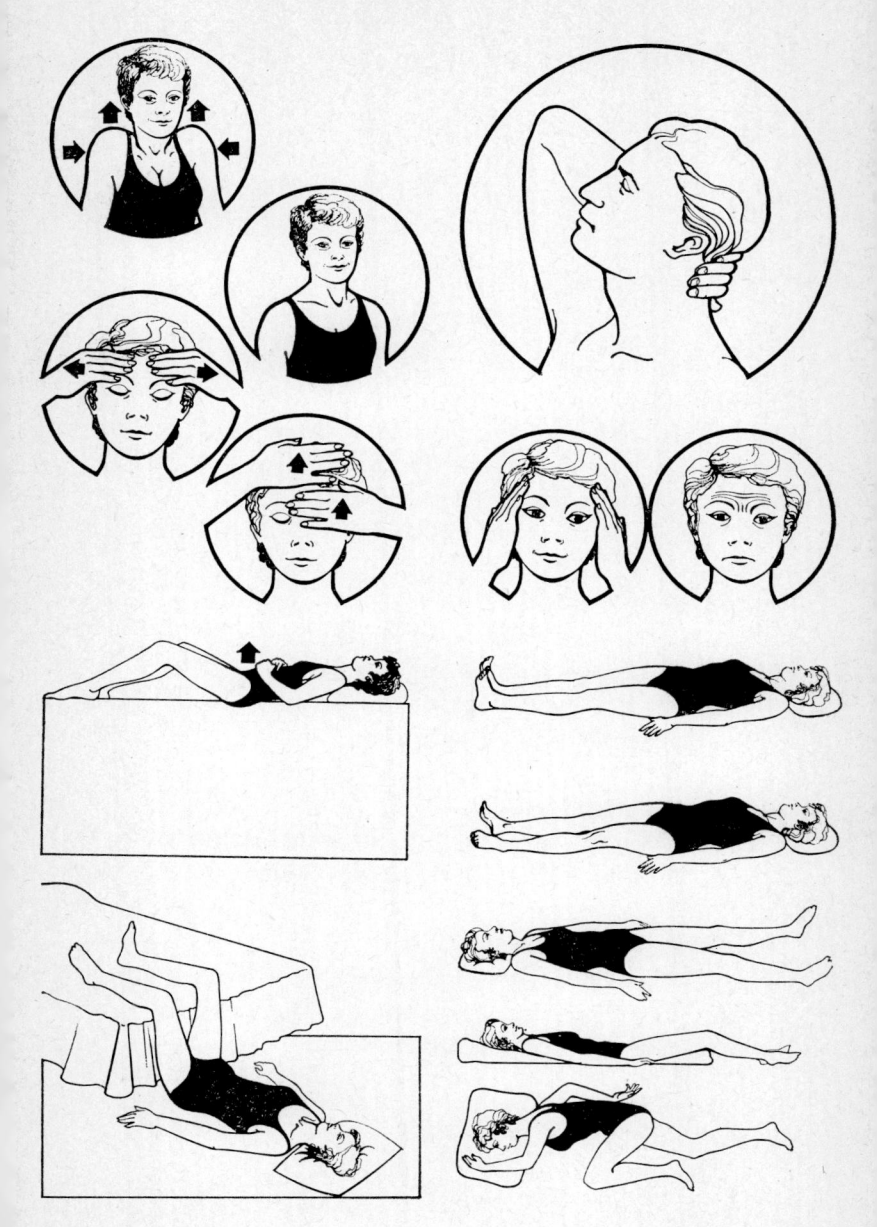

9 Book List

Relaxation
Fink, D. H. *Release from nervous tension*, Allen & Unwin
Jacobsen, E. *You must relax*, McGraw Hill
Mears, A. *Relief without drugs*, Fontana
Rathbone, E. *Relaxation*, Philadelphia: Lea & Ferbiger

Problems of women
Dalton, K. *The menstrual cycle*, Penguin
Hilliard, R. *Women and fatigue*, Pan
Landau, M. E. *The change of life*, Family Doctor series: British Medical Association

Posture and tension
Hearn, E. *You are as young as your spine*, Heinemann
Barlow, W. *The Alexander Principle*, Gollanz

The physiology of stress
Cannon, W. *The wisdom of the body*, New York: Norton
Morgan, C. *Physiological psychology*, McGraw Hill
Selye, H. *The stress of life*, McGraw Hill